Black Moon Lilith Rising

ALSO BY ADAMA SESAY

BLACK MOON LILITH COSMIC ALCHEMY ORACLE:
A 44-Card Deck and Guidebook

The above is available at your local bookstore,
or may be ordered by visiting:

Hay House UK: www.hayhouse.co.uk
Hay House USA: www.hayhouse.com®
Hay House Australia: www.hayhouse.com.au
Hay House India: www.hayhouse.co.in

Black Moon Lilith Rising

HOW TO UNLOCK THE POWER OF THE DARK DIVINE FEMININE THROUGH ASTROLOGY

ADAMA SESAY

HAY HOUSE

Carlsbad, California • New York City
London • Sydney • New Delhi

Published in the United Kingdom by:
Hay House UK Ltd, The Sixth Floor, Watson House,
54 Baker Street, London W1U 7BU
Tel: +44 (0)20 3927 7290; Fax: +44 (0)20 3927 7291; www.hayhouse.co.uk

Published in the United States of America by:
Hay House Inc., PO Box 5100, Carlsbad, CA 92018-5100
Tel: (1) 760 431 7695 or (800) 654 5126
Fax: (1) 760 431 6948 or (800) 650 5115; www.hayhouse.com

Published in Australia by:
Hay House Australia Ltd, 18/36 Ralph St, Alexandria NSW 2015
Tel: (61) 2 9669 4299; Fax: (61) 2 9669 4144; www.hayhouse.com.au

Published in India by:
Hay House Publishers India, Muskaan Complex, Plot No.3, B-2,
Vasant Kunj, New Delhi 110 070
Tel: (91) 11 4176 1620; Fax: (91) 11 4176 1630; www.hayhouse.co.in

Text © Adama Sesay, 2023

Cover design: Kara Klontz • *Interior design:* Lisa Vega
Interior illustrations: Carlos Fama

The moral rights of the author have been asserted.

The information given in this book should not be treated as a substitute for professional medical advice; always consult a medical practitioner. Any use of information in this book is at the reader's discretion and risk. Neither the author nor the publisher can be held responsible for any loss, claim or damage arising out of the use, or misuse, of the suggestions made, the failure to take medical advice or for any material on third-party websites.

A catalogue record for this book is available from the British Library.

Tradepaper ISBN: 978-1-78817-867-9
E-book ISBN: 978-1-4019-7067-3
Audiobook ISBN: 978-1-4019-7068-0

This product uses papers sourced from responsibly managed forests. For more information, see www.hayhouse.co.uk.

Printed and bound by CPI Group (UK) Ltd, Croydon CR0 4YY

To Haja and Grandmommy: The two lionesses, and divine feminine goddesses of my lineage I had the pleasure to experience and know. I express my heartfelt gratitude to you, and may this book bring healing and liberation to you in the afterlife.

Your spiritual presence continues to guide and empower me to step into my own divine essence, to honor the sacred power of the feminine, and to advocate for equality in all its forms.

Contents

⚸

Introduction

Welcome into the cosmic power of the dark goddess, Lilith. Writing this book has been an incredibly healing journey for me, allowing me to dive back into my own dark feminine energy to write about my knowledge of this mystical energy center pulsating in space: Black Moon Lilith. My astrological work has transformed my own life, the lives of my clients, and readers of my work, and I am grateful to share what I've learned with you. Lilith is about radical self-empowerment and raw rebellion, so I want to acknowledge that I conceptualized and wrote this book on Lenape land, in New York City: a territory of people who were decimated by colonialism, white patriarchy, and land theft. This control and dominance is the central theme of Lilith's mythology, so I feel it's important to recognize the original people of this land.

This is a somewhat dark astrology book, created for those who want to heal, unlock what's blocking them, and ascend from past traumas. Please note that I discuss difficult themes like death, trauma, and life crises, so proceed with caution if those topics are triggers for you. I tap into the lives and stories of clients and notable people in the hope that it provides a template for healing for those who are going through similar situations. Be prepared to be activated or emotional while you are reading parts of this book. Remember also that astrology and alchemy do not replace licensed therapy or medical doctors, and so they should be seen as only two of the many tools in your healing and mental wellness tool kit. My intention with this work is to empower generations of people who have felt oppressed, unseen, unworthy, outcast, or labeled as "too much." It's for those who have allowed past difficulties, challenges, or traumas to consume their present, and it provides a mirror to heal and empower who you truly are. It's about healing and integrating the feminine energy on the planet that has been oppressed for so long—the energy that describes the rage, raw rebellion, and aching sorrow that erupts when we experience unfair dominance and control by the outside world.

Astrology was a male-dominated practice for thousands of years, with many interpretations, studies, and concepts contributed by men like Ptolemy, Plato, and Socrates. Women's voices weren't truly visible in the metaphysical world until the 20th century, beginning with the famous American astrologer Evangeline Adams. In tarot, we also have the British artist of the Rider-Waite deck, Pamela Colman Smith. Her major contribution as illustrator, writer, and creator of the deck was overshadowed by the male occultist who commissioned her work, Arthur Edward

Waite. She received very little compensation or recognition while she was alive for what is now the best-selling Tarot deck of all time. The way we interpret the stars has been through a mainly patriarchal lens, which can limit the perspective of the practice. Like women occultists who came before, I've written this book to disrupt astrology, adding a new layer of research and interpretation through my own lens and life perspective as a Black woman in America. I do want to acknowledge that the landscape is changing in modern astrology; now you can find a plethora of voices from different backgrounds doing astrological analysis. Here, I interpret the dark goddess through my consciousness as someone who has experienced firsthand the archetype of her myth: systemic racism, prejudice, misogyny, and sexism in America on a deep, cellular level. This work is made in the rebellious spirit of Lilith, offering a different perspective on her.

When I first began incorporating Black Moon Lilith in my astrological studies, I realized how aligned her plight is with the Black woman's experience globally. Lilith's level of oppression was embedded in my DNA and in unconscious patterns from witnessing what family members have experienced, all the way back to my enslaved African and Indigenous American ancestors. Lilith, who was punished and seen as an evil monster for asking for equality, is highly aligned with the experience of people across the African diaspora. Black women endure misogyny in their communities and families even within the diaspora, and from others, they endure racism. This book will address these realities in relation to Lilith's archetype.

Goddess energy in astrology is not niche. It is not only for women. Rather, female deities and archetypes are foundational to understanding the birth chart, and everyone, regardless of gender identity, should know them. We all have various levels of masculine and feminine energy, and the healing of the feminine is needed as we progress in modern times. Lilith is the dark feminine wounding within the collective that is living and breathing within us all, waiting to be seen, resolved, and healed. Everyone has Black Moon Lilith energy, and you've felt that energy in your life depending on how she shows up in your natal chart. She gets placed in the shadows because she may be too much for you to handle, only coming out when you've left her unaddressed and unseen for too long. This insight is meant to be read and digested slowly, and it's important to take time outside of reading this book to process, meditate, and journal, especially on topics that you may find triggering or difficult to absorb. This book is also a shadow-work tool, meant to assist in self-healing. I discuss the darkness that exists in everyone's life that tends to get swept under the rug, unaddressed. Black Moon Lilith reminds us that when we shine a light on and integrate the darkness, we become empowered creators of our own lives.

Difficult events, trauma, and death are all facets of life that we cannot control, though they impact and shape our lives. Black Moon Lilith pushes you to look at the darkness within to clear what's oppressing you and holding you back from your power. Her story can shine a light on internalized patterns of misogyny, trauma, control, and low self-worth that were embedded into us since we came into this world and have blocked out our light as individuals. As you read this book, you will start to notice internal shifts that soon will manifest in your reality. It will help strip away programming, limiting beliefs, and old patterns that have controlled you, repressed you, and prevented you from stepping into all that you truly are.

Black Moon Lilith will light the fire of empowerment within you. Allow everything that falls away to be released to create space for the new.

⚸

CHAPTER 1

The Ancient Myth of Lilith

GODS, GODDESSES, DEMONS, AND THE COSMOS

Throughout human history, astrologers and mystics have associated the planets, points, and asteroids with gods, goddesses, and other mythical deities. The ancients used divine figures to humanize and bring to life the zodiac signs and planets. Archetypes like Pluto, the lord of the underworld, and Venus, the goddess of love, are embedded into myths and legends and inform how astrology manifests in our individual and collective lives. Through deepening our connection to how these deities live within us and in the world around us, we can tap into their cosmic wisdom, power, and alchemy on earth as creators. These divine archetypes were formed over thousands of years of

observing, recording, and tracking the aspects and transits of the stars. They are a divine instruction manual on
how to navigate our lives and the soul's cosmic blueprint.

Myths are part of every ancient culture and were
passed down for generations across the world to preserve, understand, and integrate a sacred guide for
self-knowledge. Math, planetary aspects, and their patterns
are also a large foundation of astrology. Ancient astrologers gained this knowledge of the stars through tracking,
recording events, and observing patterns for thousands of
years. They observed the cycles of the moon, which align
with the cycle of a monthly period; one of the ways she is
associated with the feminine. Archetypes and mythology
are a major part of the foundation of the modern astrology
that we practice in the West today. Myths, therefore, are
allegory for how the planets affect us here on earth.

Once you know the mystical story of each of the planets, zodiac signs, and placements in the birth chart, you
can understand and analyze your astrological DNA on
a deeper level. To break this concept down further, let's
look at a well-known planet like Mars. Mars is the ancient
Roman god of war, action, aggression, sexual drive, masculinity, and competition. As Mars moves through the
zodiac and aspects other planets and points, he impacts
the facets of life that it rules over. Now, think of this as
the same for Black Moon Lilith. As she moves through
the zodiac, the ancient power struggle and dark feminine
rebellion of Lilith manifests physically in different ways
on earth.

Astrology is divine wisdom about how the universe
manifests within us and in the world around us. The gods
and goddesses are here to teach us lessons and provide
a map to our true selves in this lifetime. It's incredibly

healing to understand the why, how, and what behind your brightest gifts or deepest wounds. Through this practice of looking in the mirror, we can create aligned lives from the inside out. Understanding mythical archetypes like Lilith's or Mars's mistakes, battles, wins, and lessons can empower and transform your life. Let's dive into the depths of the dark goddess, Lilith, and uncover her mystical power.

THE DARK GODDESS LILITH

Lilith is the dark side of the feminine. She's our unacknowledged wisdom, anger, pain, and rage. She is the temptress and the provoker of the masculine. She's creative, magical, intuitive, and a force of feminine power. She represents the raw, sexual, primal, wild, rebellious, and warrior side of the feminine, and her presence can trigger the shadow of control, aggression, or misogynistic tendencies from others. Her role is to destroy, create, and transform realities through defiance and a lust for freedom. Her spirit shows up in various forms throughout ancient folklore and mythology, but she is consistently portrayed as a lustful demoness, evil sexual temptress, and wicked rebel against male dominance and authority. Her archetype appears in different cultures and in different variations, and it's associated with the night, magic, rebellion, transformation, sexual desire, power struggles, and transmutation.

Lilith is one of the oldest female spirits on record. Her earliest appearance was as the wind demoness, Lilitu, who seduced men, led them astray, and killed babies in ancient Mesopotamia. Sigils, spells, and protection amulets were created to guard against Lilitu, amplifying the fear of her energy.[1] She was viewed as a terrible mother archetype who threatened death and harm to all who crossed her path.

Another recorded variation of Lilith's archetype was a small demoness who was pushed out of her home in the tree in the ancient Babylonian poem *Gilgamesh and the Huluppu Tree*. Written on clay tablets in cuneiform, this is one of the earliest surviving pieces of literature. She is also theorized to be featured on the famous Babylonian Burney Relief (often also called *The Queen of the Night*) housed in the British Museum and dating back as far as 1950 B.C.E.[2] While we know which civilization it's from and its approximate age, we will never know the original purpose or name of the relief. It was stolen from its original site before it ended up in a museum. Some anthropologists have identified the portrait as one of a busty and beautiful Lilith, surrounded by some of her symbols—owls, lions, and the tree of life—at night. She has talons, wings, a crown, and symbols on her hand indicating goddesshood and divinity.

Her role evolved from that of an evil spirit to a human as Adam's disobedient first wife before Eve, found in early medieval Talmudic and Kabbalistic texts. *The Alphabet of Ben Sira* is one of the oldest sources we have today that portrays Lilith as the first woman and Adam as the first man. She was painted as evil, seductive, and threatening because of her defiance and rejection of masculine dominance. This was due to the misogynistic nature of the patriarchal rulership during the time when her story was included in these ancient texts, when the feminine was heavily demonized and suppressed. Women were meant to be submissive, obedient, and meek; the patriarchal religious leaders who analyzed her biblical story were in societies that were deeply oppressive of women who stepped outside of submission and toward leadership, which was seen as belonging only to the masculine particularly in patriarchally based Abrahamic religions where Lilith's legend is found. This is exemplified in the sole worship of only a male god, as well as male spiritual leaders like Jesus, Moses, or Muhammad, with feminine figures either held to a strict standard of purity like the Virgin Mary or cast out if disobedient like Lilith or Jezebel.

In this version of the story, Adam and Lilith were created equally from the dust of the earth by God. God gave them dominion on Earth and they were told to procreate. When it came time to have sex, Adam commanded Lilith to lie beneath him, as he believed she was the lesser of the two. She refused to submit and proclaimed that they were equal. She screamed the forbidden sacred name of God, grew wings, and flew off defiantly to the Red Sea. Adam prayed to God and told him that the woman he was given had run away. God sent three angels after her to warn that if she did not come back, a hundred of her children would die per day. She refused, so the angels threatened to drown her in the sea. To avoid being drowned, she lamented that if the children wore the names of the three angels, their lives would be spared. This scene links her to her earlier Mesopotamian form as a child-killing wind demon.

A religious lesson like Lilith's punishment was a way for the patriarchy to control women through fear. Depictions and interpretations of Lilith have continued to evolve from those in these ancient civilizations up through antiquity to modern times. Renaissance artist Michelangelo's *The Fall of Man* in the Sistine Chapel is theorized by some to feature Lilith as the serpent who tempted Adam and Eve in the garden of Eden. This is because the serpent appears to be half woman and half snake. She was acknowledged as Adam's first wife in Victorian-era literature like *Faust*, and artist Dante Gabriel Rosetti painted her as a beautiful and seductive femme fatale in *Lady Lilith*.

The tides, however, are turning. Today, Lilith is praised as a powerful, dark feminine archetype and revered in modern divination, joining the ranks of similar transformative, magical, destructive, and rebellious dark mother archetypes like the Hindu Kali Ma, Celtic the Morrígan, Greek Hekate, or Egyptian Isis. She has been incorporated into modern pagan practices like ceremonial magick and Wicca, and was introduced into Western astrology during the early 20th century. Today, mystics, sages, witches, and astrologers are tapping into the power of previously taboo dark goddess deities like Lilith and using her story as magic and spiritual alchemy to heal themselves and the collective.

LILITH AND COLLECTIVE EQUALITY

Lilith wasn't the only character in her story; Adam also played a major role in the dynamic. The mythology of Lilith and Adam is allegory for the ancient power struggle between the masculine and feminine. She represents the dark feminine polarity, who was pushed to rebellion and rage. Adam's role here can inform how Black Moon Lilith may manifest in a man's birth chart as misogyny, control, and dominance of the feminine. Adam's esoteric symbolism can also be extremely healing knowledge if you have heavy masculine energy and want to understand how Black Moon Lilith affects you. Lilith and Adam are representations of the dark feminine and masculine, and of what can occur when they are left unhealed in both women and men. Working with the archetype of Lilith can help us all unpack and heal difficult themes in our world such as oppression, power struggles, and wars that have developed from an outdated patriarchal framework.

You can see Lilith and Adam's discordant dynamic reflected in today's world events through financial inequality, discrimination, racism, control structures, poverty, starvation, and global oppression. She triggers the protests, plight, and rage of those who are under-privileged, shunned, unequal, and unseen. Adam's drive to control and the subjugation of Lilith in the myth are powerful allegory of the dark and difficult events that manifest in society due to shadows like toxic masculinity and the ever-present patriarchy. Patriarchy is associated with violence and fear because of how it has manifested on this planet for thousands of years: in the oppression, abuse, and subjugation of women. Lilith and Adam show us esoterically that balance and egalitarianism between the masculine and feminine is the key when it comes to healing the planet.

The term *patriarchy* has nothing to do with demonizing men. I would summarize patriarchy as a theoretical social and societal system in which men dominate women and hold the positions of power. It also describes the authoritarian hierarchy that exists in male-centric organized religions. Contrary to popular belief, anthropologists have never found any purely matriarchal societies. Humanity hasn't experienced matriarchy. We have had matrilineal cultures (where lineage passes through the mother) and ancient goddess worship, but men were still in the dominant leadership roles. In turn, the world was built for the comfort of a small percentage of the collective.

Women can hold power even in a patriarchy, but they must assimilate to, champion, and further its agenda or face punishment. There is little room for female sovereignty, and if a woman steps out of line, she is cast out and labeled as rebellious, defiant, and just "too much." If women born into these institutions don't submit and comply with control, they are cast out or labeled as evil just like Lilith. The story of Lilith helps us understand the patriarchal wound that has oppressed humanity, and how we can empower the world to bring true equality for all.

The framework for today's modern society ramped up during the industrial revolution which took place during the 18th through 20th centuries, when we moved away from a slower, agrarian way of life toward mass-production. This groundbreaking era of transformation in human history aligned with the last time Pluto was in Aquarius—from 1777 through 1798. There were the American and French Revolutions, to name a couple of famous events aligned with this astrological cycle that marked a time of social, governmental, and industrial revolution. Pluto will be back in Aquarius from 2023 to 2044, and we will experience a more intense reckoning with the unsustainable societal structures that continue to oppress many while uplifting an elite few.

During the industrial revolution, human value was heavily based upon production and output. The enslavement and genocide of Africans and Indigenous Americans was alive and well in America until 1865, when the 13th amendment was ratified and passed by Congress. This was a pivotal event that laid the foundation for how most of modern society is programmed to function today—in the exhausting pattern of a hustle-and-grind mentality. The small, elite percentage keeps its power and holds back the collective through patriarchal family dynasties, religious structures, political power, and governmental laws. Most financial interests, funding, and political attention go toward fueling the elite's own agendas versus actually caring for citizens. As a result, most of humanity has been trapped and left powerless, unsupported, and living in survival mode to the present day. This is changing as the collective wakes up to its power and questions the current way of life with Pluto's revolutionary move back into Aquarius.

The United States itself is an example of how the patriarchal values of power struggle, dominance, and control were built into the fabric of a country. There is a deep wound there from slavery that must be healed and reckoned with. The country was built on genocide, theft, and violence against the native, indigenous tribes and enslaved Africans. All of this was initiated and executed by patriarchal forces like the English Crown and the Catholic Church. From mass genocides like the transatlantic slave trade and the colonization of indigenous populations across the world to the Holocaust and World War II, all of these crimes against humanity have been committed by patriarchal systems. This horrific history is the framework and structure of the society that modern Americans, including the descendants of those persecuted, must survive in today. Capitalist values are championed and held up in Western countries as the standard for excellence. The systems in place force us all to conform to them while creating inner turmoil and depression in those who don't fit the mold.

The patriarchy is not a wounding only in Western culture. Across the world in Africa, South America, the Middle East and Asia, honor killings, murderous morality police, genital mutilation, rape, and femicide are just some of the horrific atrocities and persecution women still face. Brave young women in Iran are fighting for freedom from oppression and violence against women by the morality police. Our society has been dominated and controlled by unbalanced dark masculine ideals like competition, aggression, control, dominance, racism, and violence that have harmed people in all walks of life.

However, boys and men are also hurt and damaged by the patriarchal systems that run the world. They are suffering because they don't have a stable support system or resources to build their lives so they feel aligned and fulfilled. Across the world, you can see societies dominated by masculine force and violence, and controlling, oppressive regimes. The cost of living is oppressive to many in modern times, while salaries have not matched it. Men's emotions and vulnerability have historically been shunned, leaving them to heal and handle their traumas in silence for fear of appearing weak, while violence is seen as power. We can see this reflected in difficult statistics from the Centers for Disease Control (CDC), like young men committing suicide at four times the rate of women in the United States. We are out of alignment, and it's time to balance and heal both the masculine and feminine to shift this harmful dynamic.

Lilith's myth is relevant, and the stigma around her image is shifting as people continue to step into their individual power during the cosmic shift into a new age. The world is waking up to patriarchal oppression in the 21st century as we move into the self-empowered Age of

Aquarius by waging protests, quitting corporate structures, and speaking out against the corruption in governments that are leaving people neglected for personal gain. Pluto in Aquarius from 2023 to 2044, I believe, is a major trigger of the world's entrance into the Age of Aquarius.

According to astrologers, we are stepping out of the age of religion, illusion, and suffering—Pisces—and into that of enlightenment, revolution, and innovation in Aquarius. This is the 24,000-year cycle called "the precession of the equinoxes" in tropical astrology (detailed further in Appendix 6). Humanity has experienced the Pisces religious age for the past 2,000 years. Aquarius will bring in science, innovation, individual freedom, and humanitarianism. Many astrologers believe the Aquarian age technically begins around the year 2100, meaning that we are in the transition stage during this century.

☽

CHAPTER 2

The Astrology of Black Moon Lilith

BLACK MOON LILITH

Black Moon Lilith is not a planet or asteroid; rather, she is an astronomical calculation called a *lunar apogee*, associated with the furthest point of the orbit of the divine feminine mother moon. The lunar apogee is defined as the farthest point in space on the moon's elliptical orbit around the earth. When the moon is at apogee, it also visibly appears smaller in the sky, aligning with the interpretation of Black Moon Lilith as the antithesis of the nurturing and maternal moon. In modern-day astrology, this powerful and dark hypothetical vortex in space is integrated into the birth chart along with the major planets, asteroids, and points.

A scientific fact: the moon is involved in controlling the ocean tides on earth, and when it is at the lunar apogee, there is less gravitational pull, increasing the range between high and low tides. Therefore, rough and intense water is one of the most physical manifestations of the moon forming a connection with Black Moon Lilith. We will discuss the affect of Black Moon Lilith on the moon in Chapter 6. Astrologically, water is feminine and connected with the human power of emotion. Metaphysically, we can compare the moon's effect on the tides to the raw, wild, and rebellious emotions of the dark goddess Lilith in all her variations of form from demon to first woman.

The glyph used for Black Moon Lilith is a crescent moon with a cross. This is her symbol and how she is identified in an astrological chart. All astrological analysis in this book uses the Placidus house system to analyze Black Moon Lilith placements in the birth chart. You can see her symbol and find out more information about Placidus in Appendix 5.

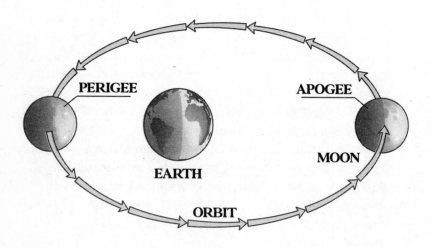

There are two calculations of the Black Moon Lilith used in astrological analysis: the mean and the true. The mean is the average movement of the lunar apogee over time. It takes approximately nine years for the mean Black Moon Lilith to move through the entire zodiac, and she also spends around nine months in one zodiac sign. On the other hand, the true calculation of the Black Moon Lilith takes the variation of the moon's elliptical orbit into account. This is the calculation of the lunar apogee, the Black Moon Lilith, at a specific moment in time.

You may be asking, which is the best calculation to use, and when? Opinions differ on this in the study of astrology. According to my own research and use of the Black Moon Lilith, I recommend the mean position for mundane astrology, and predictive forecasts like the widely popular written horoscopes based on sun signs. Typically, there are a set of 12 forecasts for each zodiac sign, and this is a popular medium in modern magazines and on social media.

While the word *mundane* can have a negative connotation, it means something completely different in astrology. Derived from the Latin word *mundus*, meaning "the earth" or "the world," it refers to the branch of astrology relating to world events, politics, history, laws, and society. Mundane astrology allows us to understand how the movement of the cosmos affects collective humanity, large generational cycles, and the planet.

True Black Moon Lilith is the best calculation for when you want to analyze a natal chart, relationship compatibility, and transits, since it gives a more accurate and detailed interpretation for a specific person. Natal astrology focuses on interpreting a person's natal chart, also called a birth chart, based on their birth date, time, and location. A natal chart is a snapshot of the sky at the exact moment and location of a person's birth, and an analysis of the positions and aspects of the planets, the sun, the moon, and other celestial bodies. Transits refer to the movement of the planets in the sky in relation to the positions of the planets in an individual's birth chart. Transits are a fundamental tool used by astrologers to understand and interpret the influence of planetary energies on a person's life at a given time. They can be a predictive tool or used for self-awareness, and you may recognize transits if you've had a personal reading from a professional astrologer.

In astrology, the moon is a luminary representing the mother, pointing to our internal world, emotions, comfort zone, ancestry. A luminary in astrology is defined as a natural, light-giving body and also a person who has reached prominent status and influences others. The sun and moon are the only luminaries in astrology, because they emit light and are the most powerful and personal parts of the birth chart. Black Moon Lilith, as the farthest reach of the moon, is therefore the antithesis of this nurturing luminary, based on her portrayal as a terrible mother in her mythology.

The number nine, the approximate cycle of mean Black Moon Lilith, also aligns with Lilith's mystical role as the dark mother of creation. Nine months is, of course, also the gestation period before the birth of a child. The human gestation period is a physical representation of internal alchemy: transmutation through darkness, life, and death. While this is more of an esoteric interpretation of the allegory and not an astrological one, it adds more layers to the interpretation of Black Moon Lilith's energy.

Think back to one variation of Lilith's myth and the curse from God and Adam of having to witness a hundred of her children dying each day due to her rebellion against their authority—not to mention her portrayal as an evil seductress and child-killing demon prior to this. Lilith is the feeling of pain, transformation, blood, beauty, and magic when the mother is about to push her creation into the world.

Rebellious, often deemed to be "too much" or "hard to handle," Black Moon Lilith is the cosmic, dark, wild child of the moon. Especially if the dark goddess is prominent in your chart, like forming connections with the ascendant, sun, or moon, her energy can make you too much or difficult for others to accept fully. Black Moon Lilith is only hard to handle for those who don't want to face the truth of who they are. She shows you your deepest fears, self-limitations, and what has been holding you back from your rawest and truest self.

As the Black Moon Lilith transits, she pulls back the veil and allows you to face and alchemize inner demons. She seeks to nurture you through empowerment, ego death, and reconstruction. She shows you what you have been sweeping under the rug and forces you to cut ties with what no longer serves. The Black Moon Lilith encourages you to surrender and accept who you are or succumb to an extremely uncomfortable transformation. She moves through the zodiac signs and connects with the other celestial bodies; her energy takes on different forms and manifests in various areas of life.

ESSENTIAL DIGNITIES

In astrology, essential dignities detail the strength or weakness of a planet in a zodiac sign. It's one of the many layers of interpretive information when looking at an astrological chart. *Detriment, domicile, exaltation,* and *fall* are four classifications I have heavily researched in regards to Black Moon Lilith. Since Black Moon Lilith was adopted by modern astrology, there has been a plethora of proposals by astrologers on the topic; consider these my beliefs as the result of my own research and work. Since Black Moon Lilith also is associated with the moon's orbit, it's only natural for her to be in domicile, or comfortable, in the moon's opposite rulership. She is the dark opposite of the reflective, luminary moon. Black Moon Lilith is in domicile, at home and comfortable, in the sign of Capricorn, and in detriment, or has a challenging experience, in Cancer.

Why? Cancer rules over tradition, family, the home, comfort, emotion, and nurturing. The moon rules over Cancer and represents women, matriarchy, and instinctual emotions. Black Moon Lilith can create turmoil in all these emotional foundations of life. Not receiving or being starved of these essential parts of early life can create internal storms, instability, and difficult emotions.

Black Moon Lilith is in exaltation in Scorpio and is in her fall position in Taurus. *Exaltation* is when a planet is the most powerful and gains strength in a sign. *Fall* is the opposite and it can prove to be more challenging. Scorpio represents death, rebirth, and intuition, and it is the darkest feminine sign out of the rest of the zodiac. Black Moon Lilith can manifest powerfully, for better or worse, in the watery depths of Scorpio.

Lilith as an archetype is the dark feminine and can handle the change, transformation, upheaval, and alchemy that is required in the sign of Scorpio. In exaltation, however, she is even more polarizing to others, and your personal growth can manifest from difficult events or trauma. While this is a heavy place to have the dark goddess, it is the most rewarding when alchemized and healed.

On the other hand, Taurus is the complete opposite of the darkness that Scorpio represents. Ruled by the goddess of love and material wealth, Venus, Taurus is abundance, fertility, and the sensual pleasures of life. When Black Moon Lilith is here, she is not used to all the wonder life can hold. There is a sense of lack and negative emotion about receiving and your value. We will discuss all of these Black Moon Lilith placements in more detail in the following chapters.

OTHER FORMS OF LILITH IN ASTROLOGY

While this book focuses on the research and interpretation of Black Moon Lilith, there are other abstract cosmic forms of Lilith in astrology I want to mention. They offer another layer of interpretation of Lilith and how she manifests in astrology. The Dark Moon Lilith, also called the Waltemath Dark Moon Lilith, is the hypothetical second moon of Earth. The mystery and confusion involved with its alleged discovery and study aligns heavily with Lilith's myth and who she is as a deity.

The Dark Moon was first allegedly spotted by astronomers in the 17th century. Named after a German astronomer who claimed to discover it (again) toward the end of the 19th century, Georg Waltemath, Dark Moon Lilith is said to be invisible because it absorbs light instead of reflecting it. According to records of Waltemath's research, it was supposedly smaller and dimmer than our actual, visible moon. He also calculated that every 177 days, the Dark Moon would pass between Earth and the sun.

Waltemath claimed that in 1898, according to his calculations and research, the second moon should pass over the sun, physically proving its existence. His discovery was dismissed due to lack of witnesses. Around 1918, famed British astrologer and published writer Walter Gorn Old, whose pen name was Sepharial, gave this mysterious moon the name and association with the biblical archetype of Adam's first defiant and demonic wife, Lilith. Naturally, this archetype was interpreted through his own lens as an Anglo white male.

Dark Moon Lilith is the more mysterious, hard-to-control, destructive, explosive, and ruthless side of Lilith. I interpret her in the birth chart as the stage of Lilith's mythology where she refuses to submit and return and, as a result, was cursed and punished by God. This is the explosive rage, sadness, and internal betrayal that she felt when reclaiming her sovereignty.

If both Dark Moon Lilith and Black Moon Lilith are together, it can amplify Lilith's themes further in the natal chart.

Nelson Mandela, late South African president and freedom fighter against apartheid, was born on July 18, 1918 in Mvezo, South Africa. He has Dark Moon Lilith, true Black Moon Lilith, and Mars in Libra forming a connection together in his natal chart. Mars (also in its debility in Libra) is the planet of war, fighting, and battle, while the zodiac sign Libra represents justice, equality, and the legal system. Both Dark Moon Lilith and Black Moon Lilith are activating Mars in Libra, indicating Mandela's role as a complete disruptor who was demonized by the oppressive and controlling systems in South Africa—like Lilith. After he was arrested by South African authorities in 1962, he was subsequently sentenced to life imprisonment for planning to overthrow the government with violence. He ended up spending over 27 years in prison before he was released in 1990, going on to become the country's most beloved president. You can see in Mandela's story how the Dark Moon amplified the passionate frequency of the Black Moon Lilith, taking her effects a harsher step forward.

Based on the cycles of the Dark Moon Lilith in ephemerides created by Ivy M. Goldstein-Jacobson and Delphine Gloria Jay, Dark Moon Lilith orbits the earth every 119 days and spends 10 days per zodiac sign, and she's always in direct motion.[3] You can use astrological resources like an ephemeris to see where the Dark Moon Lilith is in your natal chart; look it up by your date of birth. In astrology, an ephemeris is a table or booklet that provides the positions of celestial bodies (such as planets, asteroids, and comets) at specific times, usually on a daily basis. These positions are given in terms of celestial longitude and latitude, and they allow astrologers to calculate the positions of the planets and other celestial bodies relative to Earth. Some ephemerides may also include additional information, such as the phases of the Moon, the times of eclipses, and the dates of planetary retrogrades.

Asteroid Lilith (asteroid 1181) was discovered on February 11, 1927, by astronomer Benjamin Jekhowsky in Algeria. Asteroid Lilith is in the asteroid belt between Mars and Jupiter. According to my research, Asteroid Lilith is the physical culmination of the shadow transmutation that occurs through the experience of Black Moon Lilith in the natal chart. It's also an example of what can manifest if Black Moon Lilith isn't integrated and healed. While it is an extreme example, Marilyn Monroe's chart helps explain how the asteroid and Black Moon Lilith work together.

Marilyn Monroe was a natal true Black Moon Lilith in Leo in her first house of self and personality with the dreamy planet of illusion, Neptune. This manifested in her persona through the way she was perceived and treated as an international sex symbol. Her appearance put her at center stage from a young age. While working in a factory, she was discovered and hired to do pin-up modeling, and this began her career. Asteroid Lilith (1181) is in Marilyn's tenth house of career in the sign of beauty, indulgence, and self-worth: Taurus. This is forming a hard connection called a *square* with her natal Black Moon Lilith in Leo. On top of this, Asteroid Lilith here receives influence from malefic fixed star Algol. I discuss more about aspects in Chapter 6 and what malefic means in astrology in Appendix 3. Monroe's life path, public persona, and career was filled with the glitz and glamour of Hollywood, but it also covered up a difficult childhood, family, and personal life. Her life ended tragically in an alleged overdose.

Regarding the fixed star Algol: In astrology, fixed stars are not the zodiac signs. They are constellations that never move and hold specific meaning in the birth chart. According to *Brady's Book of Fixed Stars*, Algol (26° Taurus) is located on the head of Medusa, another dark goddess, who is known for her deadly head of snakes that would turn anyone who looked at her into stone. In her myth, the demigod Perseus slayed her, and in the Perseus constellation, he is holding her head. The explosive feminine rage and rebellion of Lilith is also linked with this malefic fixed star.

☾

CHAPTER 3

Black Moon Lilith Rising

Black Moon Lilith shows up in everyone's birth chart, but her potency and how she manifests varies for each person. For some, she can manifest as a minor roadblock in one's life journey; for others, she is an everyday life. When you are a Black Moon Lilith Rising, the rebellion, unconventionality, magnetism, seduction, ego death, and destruction of Lilith's mythology is extremely visible in events in your life, how you interact with others, and in your personality. You are a walking archetypal expression of Lilith, Adam, and their chaotic power struggle. There is the dark masculine side of the archetype influencing behaviors like control, misogyny, and violence, describing Adam's behavior in the myth. And then there is the dark feminine manifestation on Lilith's side, with themes of control, oppression, and subjugation by the outside world.

Astrologically, one of my requirements for a Black Moon Lilith Rising is having Black Moon Lilith in your first house of self, identity, and personality. She adds strength if she's forming a conjunction with the first angle of your chart called the *ascendant*, also called your *rising sign*. We will discuss this important aspect called conjunction further in Chapter 6. I use the Placidus house system to determine this, so in some charts, the ascendant can be a different sign from your first house, depending on its degree and the time you were born. This is the most personal place to have Lilith because your ascendant or first house of self is the most visible to the outer world and affects how you view your life experiences.

To know if you are a Black Moon Lilith Rising, you must know your birth time in addition to the date, year, and location of your birth. This is what determines your ascendant, or rising sign, in astrology and the structure of the houses in your natal chart. Astrologically speaking, the ascendant is the sign that was rising at the eastern horizon at the time of your birth. This is your personality and the mask you wear as you navigate the outer world. It's how people perceive you when they first meet you, and it represents how you show up in the world. It's the most visible part of your personality, so when you have planets or placements here in your birth chart, their energy is extremely present in your identity. If Black Moon Lilith is in this important area of your natal chart, her archetype is present, and your life experiences can mirror the experiences in her myth. This can manifest in different ways depending on your chart and what zodiac sign Lilith is in. (I recommend using the true calculation for birth chart analysis of Black Moon Lilith, as mentioned in Chapter 1.)

Someone with such an intensely passionate, polarizing, and magnetic deity like Lilith in their personality will attract similar themes from the mythology into their life. It seems as if you're either loved or disliked at first meeting; there is no in-between, and you tend to get along with others who are also black sheep. Some would say you are unapproachable. Perhaps you've undergone trauma, oppression, and challenges in your life that have made you who you are. When you've healed from the past, you use this dark energy and transmute it into creativity, art, self-expression, or your life's passion. If you allow the darkness of Black Moon Lilith to reign and take over your life, it keeps you in self-defeating, destructive, and limiting patterns versus empowering you. You are either one of the movers, shakers, and revolution-makers of society, or you're on the opposite, darker end and try to dominate or extinguish the light of others.

THE LIVES OF BLACK MOON LILITH RISINGS

The term *Black Moon Lilith Rising* was inspired by a combination of hundreds of client consultations, my own life experience as a Black Moon Lilith Rising, my research of world events, and my interpretations of the birth charts of notable individuals. I developed the archetype and coined the term because I feel that individuals whose lives are deeply influenced by Black Moon Lilith energy deserve their own dedicated manual and guidance. My intention in this chapter is to provide the self-empowerment, wisdom, and guidance I wish I had growing up as a Black Moon Lilith Rising. If you are a Black Moon Lilith Rising or know and love someone who is, this is the guide to understanding yourself or others on a deeper level.

The life path of a Black Moon Lilith Rising isn't easy, with difficult events, trauma, and challenges thrown your way. The key is to extract the wisdom from this darkness, alchemize your shadow, and channel it all into self-empowerment. In client sessions, I would notice when someone had this in their chart, and it would turn into one of the most important parts of their reading. To make things easier, I eventually started to say, "You're a Black Moon Lilith Rising!" when I saw this placement in their chart. I would go on to interpret further and mirror back to them how this dark goddess archetype shows up in their life and personality, triggering transformative aha moments, self-empowerment, and healing.

One client, whom I will call Khadijah, is a Pisces sun with a Leo moon and 28° Aries rising. Her Black Moon Lilith is in Taurus in her first house of self, forming a conjunction with expansive Jupiter. She consulted me after attending a presentation at an online conference I gave on Black Moon Lilith. As a Black Moon Lilith Rising in Taurus, Khadijah felt shame in the past and present around her physical appearance, weight, and food, and had low self-worth. Growing up, she felt creatively suppressed by her mother, and it was clear that that constant criticism was still causing her to dim her own expression in adulthood. These are all common themes with a Black Moon Lilith placement in Taurus in the first house of self. For Khadijah, the best way to transmute this dark feminine energy and shift doubt, shame, and guilt was to embrace and embody radical self-love. Channeling pain into art is an incredibly healing outlet for this placement.

Nikita, another Black Moon Lilith Rising client, was going through a painful divorce and sought me out for guidance. She is a Libra sun with a Pisces moon and 17° Sagittarius rising. She has Black Moon Lilith in the zodiac in the sign of Capricorn along with the north node, unstable Uranus, and escapist Neptune in her first house of self. Nikita's Libra sun (a relationship-driven sign) is in her paternal career house, forming a harsh square aspect with Black Moon Lilith. The north node indicates your life purpose, but Uranus and Neptune close by can bring instability, dissolution, and a desire to escape it.

Nikita's experience was deeply aligned with the astrological meaning of her birth chart. Her soon-to-be ex-husband hadn't been meeting her emotional needs; he was distant, unsupportive, and unavailable, and on top of this exhibited symptoms of alcoholism. They ran a business together, and he continually escaped his duties. Capricorn represents the patriarch, structure, discipline, work, hierarchy, and authority. Black Moon Lilith creates power struggles, suppression, and difficult hurdles in related areas of life. All this astrology was pointing to a life pattern and shadow of attracting men who didn't respect or honor Nikita. It was healing for her to turn the situation inward and identify where she had not honored her own emotions or set boundaries in relationships with men.

NOTABLE BLACK MOON LILITH RISINGS

Understanding how the experience of a Black Moon Lilith Rising manifests in public figures' lives will give you a deeper understanding of this astrological archetype. We touched on Marilyn Monroe earlier. Let's take a closer look at this timeless Hollywood icon from the 1950s and '60s, who was a Leo rising, Gemini sun, and Aquarius moon. Her true Black Moon Lilith in Leo formed an extremely close connection with her ascendant, which I've noted is also known as one's rising sign.

Marilyn Monroe was born Norma Jeane Mortenson (later called Baker) on June 1, 1926, at 9:30 A.M. in Los Angeles, California. She had an extremely difficult childhood with 12 different foster parents and was even in an orphanage. Her mother was in and out of mental institutions, leaving her completely alone in the system as a child. While hers is an extreme manifestation of the loss of childhood innocence and growing up fast, these themes are common with Black Moon Lilith in Leo rising placements.

Not only does the zodiac sign Leo rule over the spotlight, center of attention, and performing, it also is associated with childhood, play, and fun; Black Moon Lilith, though, creates a shadow around these necessary aspects of early development. When Marilyn was about to be thrown out of her final foster care situation, she ended up marrying her first husband, a 21-year-old police officer, to avoid being forced back into the orphanage. She was just 16. After she was discovered, she divorced him. She went on to become a beloved celebrity—remember, she was a Leo rising—until her tragic and untimely death by overdose at age 36. This is the age that coincides with her fourth Black Moon Lilith return, which we will discuss in Chapter 6. Her image, likeness, and name still generate excitement, wealth, and entertainment.

American treasure Coretta Scott King had Black Moon Lilith in Libra in her first house. She was a Libra rising, Taurus sun, and Pisces moon. She shared her husband—civil rights leader Dr. Martin Luther King, Jr.—with the entire nation, sacrificing herself and her family to gain equality for Black people in America in the 1960s. Alongside him, she helped lead the rebellion against segregation and racism. It's said that in her wedding vows with King, she had the promise to obey her husband removed from the ceremony. Libra represents equality, justice, and the legal system, which she challenged and turned on its head in the United States alongside her husband. It also represents relationships and love, and as such, their civil rights work was the main focus of their marriage. Even after his assassination in 1968, she continued on to fight for justice and equality in America, exuding the warrior goddess energy of Black Moon Lilith in Libra.

Another famous Black Moon Lilith Rising is talented performer RuPaul. RuPaul is a Gemini rising, Scorpio sun, and Scorpio moon. He is a late-degree (29°) Gemini rising, with his Black Moon Lilith in Cancer and Mars influencing his first house of self, identity, and personality when using the Placidus house system. RuPaul is a world-renowned drag artist with an internationally acclaimed television show that has completely challenged and progressed gender norms in society. In an interview, RuPaul revealed that his father was not around for him or his family due to his gambling addiction, and he was closest to his mother.

Cancer rules over the mother, home, and the emotional world. When Black Moon Lilith is here, you can experience emotional imbalances when it comes to your parents, family traditions, lineage, and the home. While RuPaul's mother was his biggest supporter, he has also mentioned that she held many grudges, resentments, and secrets. He said he also struggled with this like his mother, and letting things go has been extremely difficult for him.

Loss of the father or paternal relationship can be a theme with Black Moon Lilith rising. Throughout his life, he said that he would gravitate toward men who were emotionally distant like his father was, a pattern he learned from his childhood.

Spanish Cubist painter Pablo Picasso, active in the early 20th century, was a Leo rising, Scorpio sun, and Sagittarius moon. He is one of the greatest artists of all time and is a Black Moon Lilith Rising in the creative and expressive sign of Leo. However, Picasso is an example of the unintegrated dark masculine expression of Black Moon Lilith in men, which can take on the patriarchal dominance and misogyny associated with the archetype of Adam. There is a dark shadow of womanizing, bullying, misogyny, and toxic masculinity accompanying the genius of his artistic work.

How he treated the women in his life was first detailed in the memoir *Picasso: My Grandfather* by his granddaughter, Marina Picasso. This was the first book to show the dark side of Picasso. "He submitted them to his animal sexuality, tamed them, bewitched them, ingested them, and crushed them onto his canvas," she wrote. "After he had spent many nights extracting their essence, once they were bled dry, he would dispose of them." Two of his lovers ended up taking their own lives, likely driven by Picasso's ill treatment of them.[4]

MY BLACK MOON LILITH RISING JOURNEY

I created this book to uncover and analyze the astrology of Black Moon Lilith. But it can also serve as a self-empowerment tool and guide to healing. Finally, I wanted to share analysis and a perspective on Lilith in astrology from my lens as a Black woman, a member of a group that uniquely experiences misogyny, patriarchy, and racism all at once (this is also called *intersectionality*). Black Moon Lilith is incredibly heavy energy, and I want to open up with you and share some of my life experiences as a Black Moon Lilith Rising in Leo. My intention isn't to dredge up the past and remain stuck in the shadow of victimhood. It's to show you how healing and working with my dark divine feminine energy transformed my life in positive ways. Whether an experience was a positive or painful one, I believe it's extremely important spiritually to honor, forgive, and release the darkness in your life so you can truly love yourself. Your shadow is just as much a part of you as your light, and once you integrate the two, you will be unstoppable.

While I have much gratitude for my life, make no mistake: I have experienced my own unique traumas, challenges, and disempowering life events as a Black woman growing up in America. It's extremely important to honor and forgive the darkness in your life so you can genuinely love and embody your true self. My intention in sharing some of my life story and how I transmuted and channeled darkness into my light, creativity, and gifts is to help provide a map for you to do the same. Understanding myself as a Black Moon Lilith Rising in Leo helped shine a light on ancestral patterns and beliefs that were preventing me from living an aligned and fulfilling life. This was a turning point in my own self-empowerment, because I was finally able to create a reality aligned with who I was rather than allow old traumas and challenges to run my life.

Leo (where my Black Moon Lilith and moon are) is a fixed fire zodiac sign representing creativity, self-expression, childhood, and leadership symbolized by the Lion. Black Moon Lilith overshadows such a prominent place in my chart with my natal Leo moon. It indicates a broken family dynamic in early life, heavy maternal influence, matriarchal leadership, family, the home, matrilineal lineage, and power struggles as an ancestral pattern. When dark goddess energy is here, power struggles, shadow, and internal transformation can occur around these facets of life. Black Moon Lilith Rising energy can manifest heavily when we are children, forming the shadows we must shift in our adulthood. How we are raised, our family dynamic, and our early home life all give rise to beliefs and patterns that end up creating our reality in the present moment. We are trapped in self-destructive loops and stay stuck, helpless, defeated, and disempowered if we don't unpack and understand what is subconsciously causing the discord around us.

I am the daughter of an African immigrant from Freetown, Sierra Leone, of the Mandingo ethnic group. Known colloquially as "Salone," the name "Sierra Leone" itself dates to the 15th century when the renowned Portuguese explorer Pedro Da Cintra bestowed the peninsula with the name "Sierra Lyoa," which translates to Lion Mountains (it's no coincidence that I'm a Leo moon). This name captured the majestic mountains that existed around the harbor. This land was already home to indigenous tribes prior to his arrival and became an enduring symbol of resilience when Freetown was established as a British colony in 1808, serving as a sanctuary for those who had been freed from enslavement. It's important to note that Sierra Leone gained their independence from the British on April 27, 1961.

The compelling narrative of liberation and defiance even found its way onto the silver screen in 1997 with the iconic film *Amistad,* which vividly depicted the gripping courtroom battle and the triumphant return of captured slaves to Sierra Leone. As I reflect upon this history, I am reminded that the flames of rebellion and the unwavering fight against oppression that courses through the very fabric of my being, encoded in my bones and DNA. This resonates deeply with my Leo Moon and Black Moon Lilith in Leo which forms a powerful trine with fiery warrior Jupiter in Aries, reinforcing an inherited spirit of strength, leadership, and the unwavering pursuit of justice.

Stories that began with "back home, we used to," or "when I was growing up," or "you do not know how lucky you have it, my dear" from the older folks in my family always pulled me back into alignment with gratitude and humility. My paternal grandmother's leadership, tenacity, and foresight was the reason why I was born in the United States, where she knew there would be more opportunity for her family in the future. My grandfather was not around, so my grandmother led the family, taking on the roles of both parents until she remarried some years later.

She sent her children, one by one to London and the United States through scholarships and education. Although mineral and resource rich, present day Sierra Leone is one of the poorest countries in the world, still reeling from the negative effects of past wars, colonial exploitation, and imperialism. If it hadn't been for my grandmother's drive, power, and wisdom, my family would not be in America and have the opportunities that we do today.

In the context of my maternal lineage, akin to many African Americans, the historical narrative lacks definitive clarity; however, we know it's a fusion of enslaved African, Indigenous American, and European heritage. This amalgamation, tragically, likely stems from the devastating legacy of rape and colonization, and its impact on the interconnectedness of these lineages. I must note that my Black Moon Lilith in Leo forms a harsh square aspect to my transformative Scorpio sun, Mercury, and Pluto. This astrological configuration heavily reflects the generational trauma and crisis of this side of my heritage. It also shows that I'm here to alchemize, change, and break these generational curses in this lifetime, using my writing and intuitive gifts as the vehicle.

A memorable matriarch on that side of the family was my great-grandmother who we called Grandmommy. I was fortunate enough to meet and know her until she passed and became an ancestor when I was around eight or nine years old. Even though the family ended up north in upstate New York, she was from Virginia. She was born during the early 1900s, at a time when black women couldn't even vote in an election, endured traumatizing racism, and couldn't even have a bank account. During her life she also suffered through infidelity from my great-grandfather who even had a child outside of the marriage. She had a difficult marriage life; something that was common in my family lineage. One disturbing and painful story I heard about her when I was much older was that she was once raped on the train from New York to Virginia. This was the world that she had to live in as an unprotected and oppressed woman of color in America, dealing with misogyny at home and from the outside world.

I was named after my paternal grandmother, Adama, a common name in West Africa. My first caretaker was her mother, my great-grandmother. Both my grandmother and great-grandmother were the leaders and matriarchs of the paternal side of my family. While I disliked my name when I was a child, I grew into loving and appreciating it. Even my name holds the energy of Black Moon Lilith: heavy, dark, earth mother, feminine, disruptive. I also later learned through esoteric research that my name also means "of the earth" in Hebrew and is linked to the mythology of Adam and Lilith as the first man and woman. This was one of the many synchronicities that influenced me to center my astrological and intuitive healing work around the dark goddess Lilith.

Lilith and Adam's power struggle and archetypes were present in my daily life and ingrained in my consciousness through the tenacity and intensity of the women who surrounded me as a child. They were like lionesses (again, linking to my Black Moon Lilith in Leo energy), except instead of receiving protection and support from the male lions, they ended up carrying the burden of the entire pride on their shoulders. In the animal kingdom, lions travel in families called *prides*. When male cubs reach adulthood at two to three years old, they must leave their pride and find another to dominate. The role of a dominant male lion is to protect the pride and surrounding areas while the lionesses hunt for food together in packs.

In my family, however, there wasn't a true masculine protector to rely on. Conflict, imbalance, and discord between the masculine and feminine was therefore rampant in my family line. Divorce, infidelity, and separation are so frequent in my family tree that it is a clear ancestral pattern—though it seems more like an ancestral curse at times.

As such, many of the women in my family had to bear both masculine and feminine roles in their relationships or marriages with men. They worked full time, went to school, and provided financially. On the other hand, they also had to lead, protect, and take charge of the children and family. Through the years, I witnessed them do all the cleaning, cooking, and household chores and take care of everyone around them. The men would not carry more of the burden in work or properly protect the family. Or, they were simply not around due to illness, divorce, separation, or, unfortunately, death.

As a result of early exposure to all this, my Black Moon Lilith Rising manifested through a jaded perspective around relationships and my femininity that grew into the shadows of relationship imbalances, feeling unfulfilled, and crushing anxiety and depression until adulthood. Because of this family pattern of not being able to rely on the masculine, I felt a disconnection with my feminine energy because I was always on hyperdrive and survival mode as a coping mechanism from my childhood. This attracted people, jobs, and life events that reflected such a disempowering story back to me. I grew up hearing stories around abuse, infidelity, lack of truth, and instability from men so much that these became ingrained in my consciousness.

Let's pause and rewind to my early childhood in the late 1980s and 1990s to first unpack the foundation of my experience as a Black Moon Lilith Rising in Leo. I'm an only child, born in Maryland in the DC metro area. Some of my earliest memories are of my beloved paternal great-grandmother, who everyone lovingly called Haja. My paternal side of the family is mainly Muslim, from Freetown, Sierra Leone, and this name originated from

the status *Hajah* which is given to female followers (*Haji*
for men) who earn that rank by going on the sacred hajj
pilgrimage to Mecca. When I was born, Haja came to live
with us in Maryland so she could take care of me while
my parents worked. She was my first best friend when I
was little, especially since I did not have siblings, and was
simultaneously like a mother to me.

Her loud laughter, large smile, nurturing, and warm
energy radiated through every room in the house. She
always wore headscarves, wraps, and brightly colored
African clothes. My African culture is definitely where
my love for color and loud clothing come from as a Leo
moon. I even remember taking *lapa*—the Krio word for
the large scarves and pieces of fabric she would wrap
around her head and waist—and using it as my security
blanket throughout my childhood and (embarrassingly)
until I graduated high school. My great-grandmother
spoke only Krio, so it was the first language I had exposure
to before I entered school. Krio (also called Pidgin English)
is an English dialect spoken in Sierra Leone and is a mix of
African, English, Portuguese, and French. It's a product of
colonialism, slavery, and the African diaspora.

Even at Haja's old age, she would get up and dance
with her cane late into the night at family parties and
events. She was always in the kitchen cooking, ready to
offer you something to eat and listen to you talk about
whatever you felt needed telling. I remember our home
was always filled with the scent of cassava leaves, jollof
rice, pepper chicken, and akara; these are just a few of the
fragrant dishes Haja would create when she was living with
us. Some of the earliest foods I ate were traditional Sierra
Leonian dishes like this, and I still love them to this day.
We would always have some family members visiting, a

party to attend, or an extended family gathering. I remember the women always ruling the family, with mothers, aunties, and grandmothers as the matriarchs. Our house was always bustling, and I clung to Haja until she left a few years in to go take care of another new grandchild. She ended up passing later in my life—when I was around 12.

After she left the home is when the darkness really started to set in and the reality of family broke and unraveled for me. My parents separated and divorced when I was around five years old. This triggered me to grow up fast and bear heavy emotional burdens at a young age, a common trait of Black Moon Lilith Risings. Moving out of the family home and the separation seemed to come overnight and without an explanation.

There are different levels and variations of trauma; it's not just about abuse, death, and war. It can come in the form of any difficult or shocking event that completely shifts your thought process and how you respond and react to the outside world. Experiencing divorce and difficult adult relationship themes were all heavy and traumatic experiences for me as a child. I remember a lot of internal misery, darkness, and sadness during that time and for a few years afterward. I internalized everything as a child, and I was emotionally neglected and not offered support through a tragic event. Therapy wasn't as sought after in the 1990s, especially in the Black community. No one checked in on my well-being or offered mental health support. It was something I mostly comforted myself through when the adults were too occupied with their own battles.

The summer after third grade, during my first Black Moon Lilith return, my mother decided that she and I would move to upstate New York, to my grandmother's house, for financial reasons. (Every nine years, Black

Moon Lilith returns to the place she was when you were born—more on that important cycle in Chapter 6.) This move came as a shock, especially as I was not told until right before it was about to happen. The move created barriers between me, the family I was leaving behind, and my father, creating a void in my life. I lost having my father in the home each day and no longer had access to the support he provided.

On top of it all, I went from the cultural diversity of the DC metro area to being one of a handful of Black kids in the whitest town in upstate New York. This also heavily links to the sense of rejection combined with the disruptive energy with Black Moon Lilith in Leo—someone who stands out from the crowd because of how they look. I was fortunate to go to one of the best schools in the area, which I also noticed was majority white; this highlighted the de facto segregation of the area. Besides being called the N-word—a horrifying experience and one that no Black child should have to go through—by a white boy on the bus when I was in elementary school, I consider myself lucky because I only dealt with microaggressions and subtle racism in my experience growing up there. I was fortunate enough to make a solid group of friends that I still have as an adult, which helped me survive the experience of not fitting in.

To say the least, it was a culture shock when I started to go to this school, but I decided to make the best of it. I made friends, played classical violin after school, went to class on time, and did well in my studies. One thing both of my parents instilled in me was the value of education—to take it seriously and go to college. Since I can remember, I also loved doing makeup, hair, and styling outfits. I loved reading about being a Scorpio and checking my horoscope regularly in the latest teen magazines; even my earliest screen names were *moonbeam* and *stardust*. An early memory of my passions is from around four or five, when I would sneak into my mother's makeup and hair products. I would try to create looks I saw on TV and have a small fashion show with myself—my Leo energy was in full expression in those moments. My creativity was a healing outlet.

At 17, I graduated high school and could not wait to get out of my hometown to go to university in another town upstate but closer to New York City. After my college graduation, I wanted to work in beauty and fashion, so I moved down to the city at 21 years old. I worked for corporate brands throughout my 20s, ultimately grinding myself into the ground. I had a mix of a beautiful time being young, free, and enjoying New York City while battling underlying anxiety and depression due to unaddressed childhood trauma. While I loved beauty and fashion, the experience of corporate life started to drain me, leaving me completely unfulfilled.

I didn't experience a real dating life until I moved away for college. I was a late bloomer in this department due to the lack of diversity and there being a small minority of Black people in the school. It's a shame that race was a reason, but it was, and I was an outcast when it came to the dating department in high school. I also witnessed imbalance, power struggles, and difficulty between the masculine and feminine my entire life, which fogged up my lens when it came to love.

In addition to feeling empty about my work, I attracted men with whom relationships started off full of excitement but ended up completely going off the rails. These men always turned out to be unsupportive, selfish, egotistical, and emotionally unavailable. The emotional unavailability in men that I experienced at that stage in my life was a reflection of subconscious patterns and beliefs of not being able to lean on the masculine passed down to me from the women in my ancestry.

At age 27, I woke up to my power through diving deeper into astrology and uncovering Black Moon Lilith in my own natal chart. This was during my third Black Moon Lilith return and first Saturn return. (Your Saturn return occurs every 27 to 30 years and is your astrological coming of age. Saturn looks at your life and levels you up through harsh lessons and reality checks.) During this time, I had a quarter-life crisis, feeling burnt out by New York and the rat race of corporate America. I moved away from New York for a couple of years to the West Coast with a boyfriend, where the universe led me to astrology. I got a job at an esoteric media brand, and that's where my deep love for astrology continued to grow. Through my change of scenery, the universe had guided me toward a path I had not known was possible. I moved back to New York after a grueling and self-empowering breakup, and there I decided to enter professional astrology school and get serious with my passion.

I went back into corporate, but the spark had been lit to eventually start my own astrology brand. I worked my job in the day, while at night and on the weekends, I pursued my mystical passion. I connected with local astrology groups to find the best class for me. There was so much I had learned from books, but I also wanted to understand the science from veterans. I met my teacher through going to groups, conferences, and meetups. I studied privately for years, and this laid the foundation for my astrological knowledge as a professional. It was through my studies that the dark goddess Lilith came into my life.

When I researched her mythology and analyzed her position in my chart, it was life-changing. I would sit for hours, analyzing my chart, meditating, and looking at important years of my life and the cycles. I was going through major shadow work, alchemy, and internal transformation as I went deeper into my astrological work. As I was seeking to heal others, I healed myself—and I knew I wanted to empower others through my method. I documented my spiritual alchemy and shadow-work process, and this is available for you to incorporate into your daily rituals too.

As I moved into my 30s, I began to see the fruits of my labor after all the inner work I had done through what was showing up in my reality. The men I attracted started to shift completely and displayed the supportive qualities that since childhood, I had been programmed to believe could not exist. My work opportunities improved when I decided to commit to a life path I'm passionate about, where I can dictate my schedule and not burn out. Manifestation and alchemy are not just about positive thinking. They're about diving down deep into the dark trenches of your soul to unlock what hidden patterns are blocking you. They're about untwisting old knots from your mother, great-grandmother, great-great grandmother, and so on—releasing their baggage so that you can embody who you truly are. When we are aligned with our true selves, it raises our frequency and magnetizes a fulfilling reality. Instead of allowing my traumas to run the show, I was actively creating the reality I wanted to live in and using my dark feminine energy to do it.

In March 2020, when everything shut down in New York City due to the COVID-19 pandemic, it was the last time I went to work in a corporate office. I went through a massive internal change where I lost my fear around money and not being able to support myself as a full-time astrologer, joining the collective shift we now call the Great Resignation. I quit my job to become a full-time astrologer that July at the age of 32; Black Moon Lilith just so happened to be moving through my tenth house of career in the independent sign of Aries. I ran LilithAstrology.com now full time and received opportunities to write and create astrology content for various magazine and digital columns at top publications. My relationships with men have completely transformed because of this life-changing action, and I began to attract support from the masculine that I didn't realize was possible. This was all through purging old ancestral trauma, stepping into my feminine power, and reclaiming my worth. When you have the courage to shift something in one area of your life, the universe will also push you into alignment in others.

Now, as I write this book with passion at age 35, Black Moon Lilith has transformed my life. If I had received this information when I was younger, the healing process would have been so much easier. I want this book to be the beacon of light for you that I didn't have, so that you stop delaying who you truly are for others. I broke through and transmuted the negative patterns and power struggles that I experienced as a Black Moon Lilith Rising and manifested an aligned life fearlessly. Let your Black Moon Lilith Rising shine: you're here to transform the world.

☾

CHAPTER 4

Black Moon Lilith
through the Zodiac Signs

Now that you have a solid understanding of Lilith's rebellious, dark feminine archetype and mythology, let's dive into the depths of the Black Moon Lilith through the 12 zodiac signs. This chapter is your essential handbook to understanding your own Black Moon Lilith zodiac sign placement on a deeper level. As the dark goddess moves through the zodiac, she takes on the characteristics and facets of the sign she is in. This is one layer of how astrologers interpret the way important planets or placements manifest in your life. Again, I advise looking at your own birth chart to identify your Black Moon Lilith zodiac sign placement.

My intention with this chapter is to shine a light on the darkness involved with this placement, as well as to encourage healing, a deeper understanding of your shadow, and self-empowerment. Of course, all of the past clients, notable figures, and celebrities I used in my astrological research also have other planets and aspects in their charts that play roles in their endurance of the sometimes-difficult manifestations of Lilith. Though I'm focusing on Black Moon Lilith specifically, don't forget that there are other reasons why some of their life events unfurled in the way they did. This chapter demystifies Lilith's general arche-typal dynamic and what the practical lessons are from my subjects' lives. Each interpretation is based on the true cal-culation of Black Moon Lilith and how she shows up in the birth chart of an individual.

BLACK MOON LILITH IN ARIES

Aries rules the identity, ego, and self. Metaphysically, Aries is known as the baby of the zodiac, representing the spark of life when humans are first born and begin to form their identity with their main awareness on themselves. Black Moon Lilith is a disrupter in this process of self-actualization, creating insecurity and dousing out the powerful fire within, especially if you have planets or placements in Aries aspecting Black Moon Lilith in your chart. Black Moon Lilith in Aries can also delay you from stepping into your empowered self or into leadership roles.

Billie Holiday was one of the greatest jazz singers of all time. Her career was active from the 1930s to the 1950s. She was born on April 7, 1915, and was an Aquarius rising, Aries sun, and a Capricorn moon. Her natal Black Moon Lilith is in Aries in the third house of vocal talent and writing, with her Aries sun influencing money and mate-rial possessions in her second house. Holiday's debilitated Capricorn moon is in her twelfth house of addiction and loss, forming a harsh connection with her Black Moon Lilith in Aries. Essentially, this is a planetary alignment that manifests a lack of stability, structure, and the loss of emotional nurturing in the home. Billie was born to a teen single mother and an absentee father, which placed the burden on her and her mother to survive alone and without support. She got into trouble and was placed in a juvenile home as a child; she was a victim of sexual assault at nine years old (which also is the year of first Black Moon Lilith return in the birth chart). When she was 16, she joined her mother in New York City, where she was discovered performing at a nightclub.

Black Moon Lilith in Aries in the third house also can be a rebellious and creative writer or voice that transforms the collective through their vocal talent. Billie, for example, channeled her darkness and pain into her creativity, but tragically, her life was cut short by a heroin overdose, in part due to what she went through as a child. One of her biggest-selling singles was "Strange Fruit," a powerful story about lynchings in the South. It was banned on many radio stations, and she received a warning from a government agency never to sing it again. But she kept singing it in rebellion and resistance, true to the vocally rebellious Black Moon Lilith energy in the third house of communication and the voice.[5]

The dark goddess Black Moon Lilith in the fiery sign of Aries can also come in the form of being vilified for your overassertive leadership, masculinity, or warrior energy. For an example, we can look to the natal Black Moon Lilith in Aries fashion journalist and *Vogue* editor in chief, Anna Wintour. She is a calculating Scorpio sun with a fiery Aries moon, dark goddess Black Moon Lilith, and purpose driven north node. When the moon is forming a connection with Lilith, it can amplify the archetype in someone's emotions and personality, especially for a woman. Aries moons have a lot of energy, but they also can have hot tempers when provoked; this can be even more intense with the presence of Black Moon Lilith. As such, Anna is well-known for her stern, femme-fatale energy; she is both feared and respected.

Aries is also ruled by the planet Mars, known for aggression, war, brutality, and physical violence from the masculine in its shadow side. It can bring out the dark form of this aggressive Aries energy, most specifically in men. Black Moon Lilith in Aries can also manifest power struggles and aggression from others, especially during childhood.

I once had a consultation with a powerful Black woman I'll call Zena. She came to me for advice on what route to take in her life path and career. Zena was a maternal Cancer rising, with her Aries sun, south node, and Black Moon Lilith centered in her tenth house of career, the area of the chart representing the mother or father, and life path. She indeed had a challenging early life with her parental dynamic; her father was abusive to her mother, and she was also the victim of sexual trauma as a child. This deeply ingrained in her a fear and distrust of men, resulting in a pattern of unfulfilling romantic relationships in her life. She also felt underappreciated and as if her leadership was being blocked at work, which I felt was connected to these early experiences. To change this difficult dynamic, I advised self-employment in the wellness space in order to tap into her healing gifts to embrace her maternal and divine feminine energy. I suggested she take a more receptive approach in relationships with men, and ask for support from the universe to make space for the healthy masculine to enter her life. She later wrote me a letter stating she's started her own business and a thank-you for transforming her life.

Black Moon Lilith in Aries can also place an unexpected burden of having to be on masculine overdrive and to lead, initiate, and overcompensate for the lack of receiving support. This can feel especially draining to people who may naturally have more feminine and receptive energy. Another manifestation is being forced to be self-sufficient and autonomous as a child. That creates the belief that you must do everything on your own, leaving you feeling depleted and unfulfilled as an adult. Having to grow up fast and take responsibility for yourself occurs often with this placement.

BLACK MOON LILITH IN TAURUS

Taurus is a feminine earth sign ruled by the planet Venus, the ancient Roman goddess of beauty, material wealth, values, and judgment. When Black Moon Lilith is in Taurus, she creates a dark film over the sensory, earthly, and material side of life. There are different ways this can manifest depending upon your own individual chart; either you place importance on your resources or have trauma around not having enough. Growing up without financial resources is one side to the story with Black Moon Lilith in Taurus. As a response to this, you can feel stuck in lack, fear of not having enough, or blaming others for your misfortune. Your mother also may have felt alone with most of the financial burden when you were growing up. Or on the other end of the spectrum, you can judge others for not being able to create as much wealth as you. Your mother also could have placed hyperawareness around finances, with self-worth equal to material wealth.

On the other hand, if you do have material resources and wealth, you can experience vilification from others around that. There also can be cycles of self-destruction, transformation, and rebirth around your finances, which can bring feelings of instability throughout your life if left unchecked. Marie Antoinette was the infamous last queen of France from 1774 to 1793, before the French Revolution, when she was executed by guillotine. Her Scorpio sun, representing death and indulgent Venus, was in the fifth house of pleasure, in opposition to Black Moon Lilith in Taurus in her 12th house of hidden enemies, loss, and sorrow. Her overspending and luxurious lifestyle were criticized by the French people, and her alleged apathy toward those suffering led to her downfall and execution during the Revolution. There is no historical proof that she said, "Let them eat cake," her famous alleged response to her subject's hunger and poverty, but the sentiment remains.

Relatedly, battles around finances and material resources in your relationships can be another difficult shadow. Power struggles surrounding money can cause breakdowns or self-sabotage in romantic or business partnerships. You also can find yourself learning tough lessons around self-worth and what you deserve when you're involved with others on an intimate or platonic level.

Taurus also represents the physical world, including our earth, climate, natural resources, sustainability, and our food. It represents our values, so Black Moon Lilith in Taurus placements tend to have rebellious political and social views, whether for the empowerment or the destruction of humanity. I consider Black Moon Lilith to be in her fall position and therefore not comfortable in this sign (I discuss this concept in Chapter 2). One empowering figure is Greta Thunberg, a young Swedish climate activist, who is a notable Black Moon Lilith in Taurus. She is a Capricorn sun, forming an empowering connection with her Black Moon Lilith. Her Black Moon Lilith is also sending tension to disruptive humanitarian planet Uranus in Aquarius. You can clearly see how her dark feminine energy manifests in her protest and rebellion against climate change in the television docuseries about her life, *A Year to Change the World*.

She is going toe-to-toe with major corporations and government organizations, constantly challenging them to change and stop putting money first, to save us from climate disaster in the future. On top of this, Taurus represents aesthetics, and Thunberg is constantly ridiculed, demonized, and belittled by mostly male political figures and media because of her age and Autism diagnosis. This points to the misogyny and hypercriticism around looks that can come up for women and young girls who have Black Moon Lilith in Taurus. She stated on Twitter in 2019, "When haters go after your looks and differences, it means they have nowhere left to go. And then you know you're winning! I have Asperger's and that means I'm sometimes a bit different from the norm. And given the right circumstances, being different is a superpower."[6]

The hyperfocus on, or even critical opinions of, beauty, creativity, and physical form can also be a challenging shadow for a Black Moon Lilith in Taurus. Let's look at a pop culture icon to understand further. American rapper and performer Megan Thee Stallion is a Black Moon Lilith in Taurus. Her name comes from the nickname "stallion," meaning a tall and voluptuous woman. She has gained a massive, worldwide fanbase and is known for her music, curvy figure, and unapologetic personal style aesthetic. Even though she has manifested success, her dark divine feminine shadow shows up in attacks on her value and self-worth. Conservative media outlets have demonized her use of female sexuality in her music, especially in her song "WAP" with Cardi B. In a public interview on *CBS Mornings*, Megan details how she was shot in the feet by rapper Tory Lanez in July 2020, which stirred controversy ultimately leading to his trial and conviction in 2022. She came out about the incident on social media, and she rightfully accused people of gaslighting her in the situation, when she was the victim. Having to constantly prove your worth, or having it denied, is also a difficult struggle for this placement.

BLACK MOON LILITH IN GEMINI

Black Moon Lilith in Gemini is the dark side of the sign of communication; if you have this placement, you likely endure hurdles before feeling liberated in your truth. In astrology, Gemini is a mutable air sign ruled by the communication planet Mercury, who is known as the cosmic verbal magician of the zodiac. It represents the two sides of the truth, duality, and as such is symbolized by the Twins. It also is how we manifest through thought and speak things into existence. The social and creative nature of speech is a major part of Gemini energy, and Black Moon Lilith can bring shadow to this area of life—meaning that you may find it difficult to express yourself there. Once you use your voice to heal and channel your trauma or challenges, you step into self-empowerment later in life through its power.

Dark literature; moody, creative vocals; and penetrating speech are facets of the vocally powerful manifestation of Black Moon Lilith in Gemini. This is an empowering facet of the dark goddess in the sign of communication. The maven of channeling dark creativity into poetry and speech was American writer Edgar Allan Poe, master of mystery and the macabre. Being born on January 19, 1809 made him a diligent Capricorn sun with a creative Pisces moon. His moon, Venus, Jupiter, and Pluto are all in a powerful conjunction in Pisces and forming a transformative square with Black Moon Lilith in Gemini. He is most known for his short stories and poems containing mystery and dark horror themes. Because he was tapped into the darker side of life with his Black Moon Lilith placement, he could channel it creatively into his brilliant works that transformed modern-day literature.

Legendary 20th-century artist Frida Kahlo was born in Coyoacán, Mexico, on July 6, 1907. She was a creative Leo rising, Cancer sun, and Taurus moon. Black Moon Lilith in Gemini in her eleventh house of groups forms a powerful connection with the artistic planet Venus and destructive Pluto in Gemini on the cusp of her professional tenth house. Venus rules over art and creativity, while Pluto represents generational wealth, destruction, and transformation through crisis. Gemini as a zodiac sign also quite literally rules local transportation and short-distance travel. Kahlo was in a bus accident in 1925—a metal rod went through her body, and as a result, she suffered serious medical complications. However, she channeled her pain and suffering into artistic expression. In her paintings, she also dealt with themes of power struggle, traumatic miscarriages, and infidelity in her marriage to fellow artist Diego Rivera. One of her most famous pieces,

The Two Fridas, even discusses the dual nature of who she is, invoking Gemini's twin energy. She created this piece after her divorce. The traumatic events of her life shaped her art. Her creative vision transcends time and space, and through her dark feminine energy in Gemini, she created timeless works that help activate human consciousness.

Modern poetic lyricist and rapper Kendrick Lamar is a Gemini sun, with artistic Venus, wounded healer Chiron, and Black Moon Lilith. In his lyrics, he deals with issues of racial justice, police brutality, economic injustice, and systemic racism. His Black Moon Lilith in Gemini has expressed and manifested Lilith's dark energy through this modern medium to trigger change in the collective. In 2015 at the BET Awards, he performed his single "Alright," which was about police brutality, while rebelliously rapping on top of a vandalized cop car. Conservative news outlets slammed him for his lyrics and inciting violence against police officers. If your Black Moon Lilith is in Gemini, you also may be considered a rebellious or intensely free thinker; others may have a love-hate relationship with your ideas and verbal expression. Your opinions may be polarizing, but they are incredibly valuable, as they have the power to trigger transformation. It's extremely important to own your voice and embrace your authentic message regardless of outside opinion. You are here to change the world.

BLACK MOON LILITH IN CANCER

When Black Moon Lilith is in Cancer, your mother, family, traditions, lineage, women, and the emotional world are transformative and powerful parts of your life, for better or worse. The zodiac sign, Cancer, is an emotional, feminine water sign ruled by the moon, invoking nurturing, emotional leadership, sensitivity, and self-protection. Its symbol is the Crab, who has a hard shell outside for security and a sensitive, soft inside. Black Moon Lilith is the antithesis of the moon, so she's in her detriment and extremely uncomfortable in the nurturing side of Cancer. If this describes your placement, you can feel cut off from essential early-life needs. When Black Moon Lilith is in this sign, there can be a disconnection, a challenging relationship with the family, or rebellion against lineage. You may also experience a role as the black sheep of the family.

On the other hand, this can also manifest with the mother as the dominant force of the family. She also can be a rebellious and unconventional woman, passing this energy down to you. Depending on your chart, this could be empowering and healthy for you, or extremely challenging; on that darker end of the spectrum, she could go through difficult power struggles and battles in her life. Let's use Malcolm X as an example. Malcolm X, born Malcolm Little, was an historic African American leader and figure in the Nation of Islam during the civil rights movement in the United States. Born in 1925, he was a natal Black Moon Lilith in Cancer, forming a connection with malefic planets Mars and Pluto. Mars represents war, violence, and battles, while Pluto is authority, crisis, and death. Both of Malcolm X's parents were civil rights freedom fighters, and this made them and their home a target of violence from the Ku Klux Klan. His father was tragically killed in a streetcar accident when he was six. This left him and his siblings under the care of his mother,

Louise Little, in poverty, until she was committed to a state mental asylum for 25 years.

As a result of her freedom being taken away by the state, Malcolm X had limited contact with his mother throughout his life. He was tragically assassinated for his activist work in 1965. A 2022 article in *The New York Times* covered the overlooked yet crucial role Malcolm X's mother played in shaping his worldview and inspiring his work.[7] She experienced similar persecution to Lilith's in her life and passed the rebellious desire to fight down the family line to her son.

Let's look at another famous natal Black Moon Lilith in Cancer: Diana, Princess of Wales, who married into the British monarchy. It's reported that as a child of divorce, she had unhappy early years, and she was often in an emotionally unfulfilling situation. On top of this, she also had a rocky and challenging relationship with the royal family and her arranged marriage to Prince Charles. Born July 1, 1961, she had a caring and family-oriented Cancer sun that was overshadowed by Black Moon Lilith, and Mercury retrograde in her seventh house of relationships. The dark goddess manifested in her tumultuous relationship with the royal family, which has been described in countless movies, documentaries, books, and articles as emotionless, without support, and without true love. She also was estranged from her own mother, which can occur with some Black Moon Lilith and Cancer placements. She was known as the "People's Princess," which also relates to Cancer ruling over the "common people," and her humanitarian Aquarius Moon, but under the dark influence of Black Moon Lilith, she also went against the traditions of the royal family. She was known for being rebellious and stepping outside of royal duties, including fighting for land mine removal in Africa.

Black Moon Lilith in Cancer can also influence you to be an alternative mother or parent—or not even want the role—which goes against what traditional societal norms dictate. You want to go against the grain and choose the lifestyle that is right for you. Some might even describe such a person as a "reluctant mother" or a woman who doesn't feel fit for the role in her lifetime.

Jennifer Aniston, an American actor whose breakout role was in the TV series *Friends* in the 1990s, has Black Moon Lilith forming an almost exact connection with the midheaven representing maternal influence and career. Her parents divorced when she was nine, coinciding with her first Black Moon Lilith return (we will discuss this life cycle event in Chapter 6) and she grew up having a difficult relationship with her single mother, Nancy Dow. They were estranged, especially during her early career, and her mother even wrote a tell-all memoir that didn't help the relationship.[8] Throughout her career, Aniston was notoriously targeted by the tabloids and media about whether she was pregnant. In a 2021 *Hollywood Reporter* interview, she opened up about her frustration with this, calling out the double standard regarding how women, but not men, are judged on marital status and whether or not they have children.[9]

BLACK MOON LILITH IN LEO

The best way to explain the zodiac sign Leo is to discuss its planetary ruler, the sun. The sun is the central life force of our galaxy, and without its life-giving rays, we would not survive on Earth. The heat it emits represents creativity, life, and light, and it shines brightly to benefit our existence. Leo is the entertainer, leader, and a fixed fire sign symbolized by the royal energy of the Lion. When the dark goddess Black Moon Lilith is in such an expressive sign, she can dim this natural light—or you might be someone who challenges the norm of what a leader should be. Leo also represents the child within, and those who have this placement tend to grow up fast due to difficult childhood events.

You can be a disruptive leader, which can either enhance or dim your light if you allow it. The 44th U.S. president—and the first Black president—Barack Obama, served two terms from 2009 to 2017. He was born in Hawaii; his mother is a white American woman, and his father was from Kenya. He was raised by his mother and the other matriarchs of his family while his father was not around much.[10] In a 2008 speech noted in *The New York Times*, you can see his Black Moon Lilith in Leo energy shining through. "I know the toll it took on me, not having a father in the house," he said. "The hole in your heart when you don't have a male figure in the home who can guide you and lead you. So I resolved many years ago that it was my obligation to break the cycle that if I could be anything in life, I would be a good father to my children."[11] He is a confident and bright Leo sun with Black Moon Lilith and communication planet Mercury forming a close conjunction in Leo. His presence alone has disrupted hundreds of years of white men holding the most powerful position in the world. On top of this, he was a polarizing figure, either celebrated for his leadership or demonized depending on what side of the American political aisle the viewer was on.

Jealousy, smear campaigns, and judgment of your creative expression and light are common themes that Black Moon Lilith in Leo placements tend to go through. You break the mold just by being *you*. Lizzo, a Black pop star, performer, and classically trained flutist, has Black Moon Lilith in Leo forming a square connection with her creative Taurus sun, vocal Mercury, and expansive Jupiter. Taurus rules over beauty standards and the physical body, and in turn is ruled by the voluptuous celestial goddess Venus. Throughout Lizzo's career, while she has had success and built a loving fan base, other celebrities, influencers, and media outlets have always been there to criticize her body, self-confidence, and pride in how she looks. She even refers to herself proudly as a fat Black woman.[12–14]

In September 2022, she received the honor of being invited by the Library of Congress to play fourth president James Madison's crystal flute—only one other person has played it since it was donated to the library in 1941. She also played it at her concert later the same evening.[15–18] It's important to note that Madison owned slaves and is also known as one of the fathers of the Constitution. He is therefore a part of—and a creator of—the patriarchal establishment in this country. As a Black woman, Lizzo received praise for participating in such a historical moment and, on the other end of the spectrum, backlash stating that she had "desecrated" history. Focusing on your authentic expression, shining your light, and ignoring what people who don't agree with you say is the most empowered way to heal Black Moon Lilith in Leo.

BLACK MOON LILITH IN VIRGO

There's no such thing as perfection, but when you have Black Moon Lilith in Virgo, you're probably looking for it, and you may hold yourself or others to an extremely high standard. Virgo is associated with the symbolic virgin Maiden, who is in turn aligned with cleanliness, purity, and perfection. Work, nutrition, physical health, and service are also in alignment with Virgo energy, but when the dark goddess casts a shadow in this sign, it can create challenges, trauma, or imbalances in this area of life. Your parents could have been extremely accomplished, giving you a lot to live up to. As a result of not feeling good enough, those with Black Moon Lilith in Virgo may restrict themselves from pleasure and certain foods or be overly critical of themselves or others. This could be your reaction to having hypercritical parents or a childhood focused on work, achievement, and keeping up perfect appearances.

Michael Jackson's daughter, Paris Jackson, has Black Moon Lilith in Virgo in her sixth house, also ruled by Virgo, representing health and work in her natal chart. Her famous father was a Virgo sun himself and grew up in the spotlight, forced to achieve perfection by his father first and then the music industry. In the 2020 documentary series *Unfiltered*, Paris revealed her struggle with body image and self-esteem, which reared its head especially when her father passed in 2009. She admitted, "I'm not even close to loving myself." Body dysmorphia or eating disorders can develop on the severe side of this placement. In an interview with friend and fellow celebrity Willow Smith, Paris explained how growing up in the spotlight placed a lot of pressure on her and negatively affected her mental health.[19] She felt constant pressure to represent her family name well in public, and in the past, this held her back from fully expressing herself. Perfection can be a deep-seated shadow that prevents you from stepping into your full power when the dark goddess is in Virgo.

With men, this placement can push them to hold women in their lives to an extremely high standard, expecting perfection that no one can realistically maintain long term. Playboy media mogul Hugh Hefner was, unsurprisingly, a masculine Aries sun with a Virgo ascendant. His imaginative Pisces moon also formed an exact connection with the exalted goddess of illusion, beauty, and romance, Venus in Pisces, in his sixth house of work and daily life. You can see this manifest in his vision for the Playboy brand, putting the women he saw as perfect up on pedestals. After his passing in 2017, some of his past girlfriends and Playmates came out and described what happened during their relationships with Hefner and their time at his Playboy Mansion. According to them, there were weigh-ins and budgets to be spent only on beauty and cosmetic surgery.[20] The manifestation of Black Moon Lilith in Virgo in Hefner shows the dark side of the placement and that holding others to certain standards can be harmful and disrespectful.

Black Moon Lilith in Virgo may also bring out the vindictive dark side in the feminine that can emerge in the quest for perfection. Let's take former competitive figure skater Tonya Harding as an example. Her Black Moon Lilith in Virgo is forming a close conjunction to the dark and destructive planet, Pluto. She grew up with a mother who pushed her hard to excel in her sport and has publicly stated that her mother was physically and verbally abusive to her. And for some time in the 1990s, she was among the best skaters in the world.

On January 6, 1994, Harding's rival Nancy Kerrigan was infamously attacked after practice in Detroit by Harding's ex-husband, who hired a hit man to violently assault her legs with a collapsible baton.[21] Kerrigan was the only skater standing in Harding's way toward joining the Olympic team, so everyone suspected Harding. In the end, she pleaded guilty to the charge of conspiracy to hinder prosecution and paid with a hefty fine and probation. She was the only one in the case who didn't go to prison, but she also lost her career and was kicked out of the U.S. Figure Skating Association. Using dominance and force cost her the achievement that she wanted so badly, though she maintains innocence to this day.

BLACK MOON LILITH IN LIBRA

Black Moon Lilith in Libra brings power struggles, crisis, and difficult shadows in relationships and legal matters. Symbolized by the balance of the Scales, Libra represents the dynamics in agreements, contracts, and the bond between two people. Venus, the ancient fertility goddess of Rome, is the planetary ruler of Libra. When the dark goddess is situated in the domain of the love goddess, it can cause discord in your relationships. The solution is to have the courage to shift restrictive patterns like codependency and investing in relationships that don't honor you, and partners that are not in alignment with you. When you do this, you lead change against the system, against the status quo. This need to deconstruct can also be a part of the dark goddess in cardinal air sign Libra.

Libra also rules over beauty, your appearance, and aesthetics. Black Moon Lilith can bring a hyperawareness to this side of life. Consider celebrity, reality television star, entrepreneur, and influencer Kim Kardashian. She has a Libra sun forming an almost exact connection with Black Moon Lilith; the planet of lessons, Saturn; and transformative Pluto in the areas of society, prosperity, career, the father, and public persona. Kim's relationships have been extremely public in the press, social media, and tabloids since her sex tape was allegedly leaked in 2007. Libra also represents the law, justice, and equality; Kardashian has been married three times, each ending in divorce. Her lineage is also deeply involved in the legal system as the daughter of high-powered attorney Robert Kardashian, who defended O. J. Simpson in his infamous 1995 murder trial. She has spent time studying law, and as such has also prioritized philanthropic work with criminal justice system reform. Feeling empowered to shake up and transform the system is a powerful manifestation of her Black Moon Lilith in Libra.

Feeling closed off from relationships, having to do the most work in one, or not experiencing love or a happy relationship at all can also be a difficult theme for Black Moon Lilith in Libra placements. Across the board in my client consultations, people who have this placement have experienced difficult situations in love. Furthermore, a history of parental divorce, or legal battles in the parents' relationship, can create patterns of self-sabotage in relationships. Black Moon Lilith in Libra can also trigger the energy of dominance, inequality, and control, most specifically in men. Chris Brown, an American R & B singer, is a Leo rising, with Taurus moon and sun. His Black Moon Lilith is in Libra in his third house of communication and the voice. In 2009, he pleaded guilty to assaulting his then girlfriend, fellow singer Rihanna, in a public domestic abuse altercation. Since Libra also represents the law and judicial system, it's unsurprising here—but still unfortunate—that Chris Brown has faced a number of legal battles, especially involving women. When facing this dark masculine shadow, it's important to shine a light on how controlling or angry behavior toward the women in your life will destroy relationships. Looking in the mirror in instances like this is one of the most challenging facets of shadow work with a Black Moon Lilith in Libra placement, because the scales have two sides in the balance of a relationship.

A unique or nontraditional point of view in the institution of marriage can also manifest. You want to be in relationships where you still retain your own sovereignty. Rejection of traditional values is a deep part of the dark goddess in Libra. Or you can have a radical view of women's value and the expectations that society impresses on them.

Black Moon Lilith in Libra can also make you a freedom fighter, someone who wants to completely shift the law or a system of government. It can trigger a life of rebellion due to deep oppression and being treated unequally by the outside world. Nelson Mandela, who was mentioned earlier, had Black Moon Lilith forming a close connection with the warrior planet Mars and forming a harsh connection to authoritative Pluto in Cancer. Both malefic planets amplified his Black Moon Lilith, and we can see this manifest through his life events. He and his wife, Winnie Mandela, mobilized as activists working to dismantle the racist apartheid regime in South Africa. This system of segregation by race kept Black South

Africans trapped in subjugation, inequality, and poverty, while white South Africans enjoyed economic advantages, health, and privilege. The government arrested him in 1962, and for 27 years he was held in prison. When he was released, he continued his fight against apartheid, eventually becoming the first president of South Africa. To this day, though, he is considered a hero in activism, defiance, and social justice.

BLACK MOON LILITH IN SCORPIO

Lilith's archetype as the dark mother is strongest, and in her exaltation, when in the dark feminine sign of Scorpio. As noted earlier, exaltation in astrology means that a planet or placement can easily manifest its full expression. Black Moon Lilith in Scorpio is both challenging and rewarding when integrated. Symbolized by the venomous Scorpion, Scorpio is a fixed water sign, which represents psychic power and the depth of emotion. Secrets, crisis, the occult, and power all live under the zodiac sign Scorpio. Mars, the god of war, and Pluto, the lord of the underworld, both rule over Scorpio. Transformation, death, and crisis are other uncomfortable parts of life ruled by Scorpio. Black Moon Lilith intensifies experiences around these already dark themes in life.

When Black Moon Lilith is in Scorpio, you may experience sexual trauma, power struggles, or crisis in your life. Gabrielle Union, a talented African American actor, is a Scorpio sun with Black Moon Lilith, and is a rape survivor. She's shared her trauma in her memoir, *We're Going to Need More Wine,* to raise awareness and help others who have gone through the same. We can also see a self-destructive version of this manifest in the life of Johnny Depp, who grew up with an abusive mother. He is a natal Black Moon Lilith in Scorpio forming an exact connection with Neptune in his fourth house of home and family. Neptune indicates the need to escape through things like alcohol or substances. He discussed his childhood trauma and substance use publicly during his 2022 defamation trial between him and former wife Amber Heard. Both Union and Depp show that you can either channel your pain into light or allow it to keep you stuck and trapped in the past. When it comes to working with the dark energy of Black Moon Lilith in Scorpio, it would seem there is no in-between.

Artists, writers, and creatives who have Black Moon Lilith in Scorpio in their charts tend to express themselves through darker stories and themes. Scorpio rules over, horror, the macabre, hauntings, witchcraft, psychic power, magic, hidden forces, and the spiritual realm. British occultist, writer, and teacher Aleister Crowley, active in the earlier 20th century, had Mercury, Black Moon Lilith, and Jupiter in Scorpio. He practiced magick, authored notable occult books, and created his own belief system: Thelema. However, he only became a well-known figure after his death.

Scorpio also rules over joint business dealings, other people's money, loans, and debts. When Black Moon Lilith is in Scorpio, she can create rebellious entrepreneurship. This is especially if she's influencing the financial second and eighth houses or forming a connection to another planet in the sign of Scorpio. Steve Jobs, Kris Jenner, Walt Disney, and Jeff Bezos all have Black Moon Lilith in Scorpio in their charts and are known for their cunning business acumen and for completely revolutionizing their industries. At times, people like these also can face scrutiny or critique on how they affect others with their strategies.

BLACK MOON LILITH IN SAGITTARIUS

Sagittarius is the ascended wisdom, higher consciousness, and expanded view that we experience once we go through the death-and-rebirth cycle of Scorpio in the zodiac wheel of life. Sagittarius is a mutable fire sign representing beliefs, wisdom, optimism, growth, global affairs, and expansion. It also is linked to theology, religion, philosophy, prophecy, and visions. Symbolized by the Archer pointing his arrow toward the infinite possibilities of the sky, it's ruled by expansive Jupiter and linked with higher perspective—the wisdom and spiritual ascension you gain through life experience.

When Black Moon Lilith is in Sagittarius, your freedom-loving energy—or, quite literally, your freedom itself—can be repressed and controlled. This trouble can relate to your religion or beliefs. Consider Anne Frank, a young Jewish girl who, during the Nazi occupation of the Netherlands in the 1940s, had to stay in hiding with her family. Her diary told her story. She was born June 12, 1929, with a Leo rising, Gemini sun with intuitive Mercury retrograde, which made her a naturally talented creative writer. Her Black Moon Lilith in Sagittarius was also in the same zodiac sign as restrictive Saturn, adding rebellion and suppressed expressive freedom to Anne's fifth house of creativity. Two years into hiding, the family was discovered and taken to concentration camps. Anne Frank and her elder sister, Margot, tragically died from typhus in Bergen-Belson. Her father, Otto Frank, was the family's only survivor, and upon reading his daughter's diary, he was so moved that he decided to publish it. It has made an incredible impact on readers worldwide.

Your love for freedom, adventure, and experience can be controlled by others, leaving you feeling restricted and depleted. Pop superstar Britney Spears experienced this with her public conservatorship battle. She testified in court, saying that her father had harmful legal, financial, and social control over her life since 2008. Britney Spears is also a Sagittarius sun with her Black Moon Lilith also in Sagittarius, forming a tight connection with foggy and secluded planet Neptune. Spears has detailed how substances and prescription medications were used to control her, a common theme of a Black Moon Lilith and Neptune conjunction.

The dark goddess can also manifest in Sagittarius through a rebellious approach to teaching and sharing your wisdom with the world. This is the archetype of a radical guru or alternative sage. Different approaches to travel and experiencing the world can also be an attribute of Black Moon Lilith in Sagittarius. In universal law and alchemy, your belief system is a part of what creates your reality. When you shift the dark energy surrounding your beliefs, you will move into creative mastery. Knowing that you are a wise, intelligent being is important to healing when you have this placement. Those who have Black Moon Lilith in Sagittarius in their natal charts can experience an unconventional approach to their spiritual or academic growth. Sometimes they can even be dogmatic, creating friction with other people.

BLACK MOON LILITH IN CAPRICORN

Structure, hierarchy, status, power, and work are all integral parts of the stern earth sign Capricorn. When Black Moon Lilith casts her shadow in Capricorn, she can spark rebellion against traditional or hierarchical structures. Capricorn is a cardinal earth sign, symbolized by the sea goat who manifests their reality through hard work, practicality, and steady determination. When the dark goddess is in this sign, it's a challenging path to the top of the corporate or business ladder, and you can constantly experience power struggles in your career. Saturn is the planetary ruler of Capricorn, representing restriction, age, and lessons. As noted earlier, Black Moon Lilith is in domicile and gains strength in the sign of Capricorn.

Aminata, a cherished client of mine, is a Capricorn sun with the north node, Black Moon Lilith, Uranus, and Neptune all centered in her fourth house of the home, roots, father, and family. She experienced these archetypal themes deeply within her life and came to me to understand the difficult relationship she was having with her child's father. She had broken up with him because he neglected both her and their child. This triggered old father wounds from her childhood and relationship with her parents. Her father was not around much, and when her parents broke up, he left. She had to deal with her mother's pain and said she was domineering, nitpicky, and not nurturing; this was a manifestation of her Black Moon Lilith in Capricorn in this area of her life. Especially if you align mostly with feminine energy, Black Moon Lilith in Capricorn can create a restrictive relationship with the patriarchy in childhood that can continue through adulthood in relationships with the masculine.

Black Moon Lilith in Capricorn paves a unique path upward. Every time you achieve or gain the status you desire, there is always someone or something there to overshadow you. As a result, you can build up fear around your own power, and you must shift this to succeed or move up in the world. Madam C. J. Walker was the first Black female multimillionaire in the early 20th century and was a beauty entrepreneur, activist, and philanthropist. She is most famous for her rags-to-riches story during a time when it was close to impossible for a Black woman to achieve the amount of wealth she did. She was born Sarah Breedlove on December 23, 1867, in Louisiana to a family of formerly enslaved people but was orphaned at age seven. Madam C. J. Walker was a hardworking Capricorn sun with beauty genius Venus, driven Mars, and independent Black Moon Lilith forming a stellium in Capricorn. A stellium in astrology is when three (some astrologers believe four) or more planets are in one zodiac sign or house in a chart. This combination amplified the hardworking nature of her Capricorn sun but also presented hurdles to the power, stability, and business growth she craved. While she did enjoy success, she had to battle racism and gender inequality on her way to the top. The company she created ended up also helping Black women find employment to build their careers and achieve financial freedom.

Challenging the system and breaking the status quo is also a powerful aspect of Black Moon Lilith in Capricorn. Consider Dr. Martin Luther King, Jr., the iconic African American leader and freedom fighter for civil rights in the 1960s who was touched on earlier. MLK Jr. was a Capricorn sun in his ninth house of religion and higher learning, with Black Moon Lilith trailing close behind and destructive Pluto in Cancer in opposition.

BLACK MOON LILITH IN AQUARIUS

Black Moon Lilith in Aquarius is the most rebellious, unique, humanitarian, and inventive of the dark feminine placements. You either embody and accept your eccentricities, or you suppress them to your own detriment because of the response you may receive from other people. It's important for Black Moon Lilith in Aquarius placements to understand that others' reactions have nothing to do with you. The key to healing this placement is to liberate your mind from others' expectations of you and express your ideas regardless of whom those ideas may trigger or bother. Aquarius is a fixed air sign symbolized by the Water Bearer, who pours ascended knowledge out to the collective. Structured Saturn and eccentric awakener Uranus are the planetary rulers of Aquarius. Friends, networks, society, groups, humanitarianism, innovation, and the collective all coincide with Aquarian energy.

When Black Moon Lilith creates a shadow in this innovative sign, your radical and humanitarian points of view can be shunned or challenged at first—until the world catches up with your forward-thinking viewpoint, making it the status quo years later. Rosa Parks, a notable Black Moon Lilith in Aquarius, was arrested after she refused to give up her bus seat to a white man in 1955, sparking the Montgomery bus boycott that year and fueling the civil rights movement that continued into the 1960s. She was an Aquarius sun, Mercury, Uranus, and Black Moon Lilith all in her first house of self and personality. This stellium explains her act of defiance. Black Moon Lilith in Aquarius is like a sudden electrical shock to the collective consciousness, bringing old paradigms, patterns, and societal constructs to their knees.

We can see a similar story—of Black Moon Lilith in Aquarius being a force of societal change that is not listened to at first—play out with former U.S. Vice President Al Gore, who is a Leo rising. He has Mars, Saturn, and Pluto in Leo in his first house in opposition to Black Moon Lilith in Aquarius, bringing resistance from others to his climate crisis work and sustainability platform. The goddess of justice, Venus, is at home in the earth sign of Taurus in his tenth house of career but forms harsh connections to Black Moon Lilith in Aquarius and his Leo placements. Together, this planetary alignment astrologically represents the hard stance he takes on environmental preservation, which is completely the opposite of modern politicians who largely ignore and delay solving this threat against humanity. He even used the creative power of his Leo placements to write a *New York Times* bestseller, *An Inconvenient Truth,* released in 2006 along with an Academy Award–winning documentary, to raise awareness on the dangers of global warming. His willingness to go against what's popular for the good of all is a strong trait of those with Black Moon Lilith in Aquarius.

Billionaire philanthropist Warren Buffett is also a Black Moon Lilith in Aquarius. He has pledged to give away 99 percent of his wealth to philanthropic causes and challenges other elites to do the same. In his official pledge letter, he states, "Were we to use more than 1% of my claim checks on ourselves, neither our happiness nor our well-being would be enhanced. In contrast, that remaining 99% can have a huge effect on the health and welfare of others. That reality sets an obvious course for me and my family: Keep all we can conceivably need and distribute the rest to society, for its needs."[22–23] His focus is on doing what he can do to help humanity while encouraging his children to do the same. This highlights a shadow in Black Moon Lilith in Aquarius men to put the ascension of humanity and large groups first—sometimes, but not always, at the detriment of nurturing their loved ones.

BLACK MOON LILITH IN PISCES

If your reality is bleak, dark, and uninspiring, you will seek to escape the humdrum of the everyday in creative and spiritual ways. The zodiac sign Pisces is a feminine water sign that represents emotion, fantasy, creativity, illusion, and escape. Symbolized by the Fish, this is the final sign of the zodiac, also associated with the sacrificial energy of Jesus Christ and the religious Age of Pisces we've experienced the past two thousand years. Pisces represents the unknown, the spiritual realm, and sacrifice. When Black Moon Lilith is in Pisces, there is the desire to escape traumas, crisis, or difficult emotions through creative and spiritual means, or, on the darker end of the spectrum, destructive ways. Transcending addiction and transforming it into a creative outlet is important for healing this placement.

Grace Jones: no further words are needed to describe this force of beauty—this raw, sexual, and creative powerhouse who rose to fame in the 1970s and 1980s. She is a star in film, music, and modeling known for her brazen fashion, scandalous parties, and avant-garde talent. She is an indulgent Taurus sun that forms an electrifying square aspect with her creatively repressed but transformative Saturn and Pluto conjunction in Leo. She was born in Jamaica in an extremely religious and controlling household, which she has said was abusive. When she became embodied in her creative path as an adult, she was able to rebel against her religious upbringing but would also seek escape through substances and sex. Rejection of standard religious doctrine for more spiritual or alternative beliefs can occur with people who have the dark goddess in Pisces.

A Black Moon Lilith in Pisces who channeled difficult addictions and trauma into empowerment for the collective is Gemini sun author, comedian, and actor Russell Brand. He is a late-degree Capricorn rising and his first house contains Black Moon Lilith in Pisces, making him a Black Moon Lilith Rising. Raised by a single mother, he had a lonely and difficult childhood, which came to plague him as an adult. Brand has been extremely public with his past of drug and sexual addiction and how he had to hit rock bottom before changing his life. In one of his books, *Recovery: Freedom from Our Addictions*, he addresses his own addictions and how he was able to climb out of their cycle. His Black Moon Lilith in Pisces forms squares with radically spiritual Neptune in Sagittarius and personal Gemini sun. As a result of this harsh planetary alignment, he experienced the destructive side of Black Moon Lilith in Pisces, when someone falls into the trap of escape and does not heal or alchemize the demons that plague them. Finding healing, serving others, and infusing spirituality into his life path has helped Brand empower others and himself.

{

CHAPTER 5

Black Moon Lilith through the Astrological Houses

Black Moon Lilith not only shows up in the 12 zodiac signs; she also casts her dark shadow in one of the 12 houses of your chart. Everyone has a unique birth chart, and your houses are determined by your rising sign or ascendant. You must know your exact birth time in order for your rising sign and houses to be as accurate as possible. This is the second piece of information you can layer onto your Black Moon Lilith sign analysis after you first identify and understand the zodiac sign placement. The houses in astrology are critical and foundational to understanding in which areas of life Black Moon Lilith is affecting you. It's also important to differentiate the sign interpretations from the houses to accurately understand your Black Moon Lilith; I do not recommend combining the meanings of the two!

There are 12 houses in the astrological birth chart, each representing certain facets of your life. Depending on where your Black Moon Lilith is placed, Lilith's mythology can manifest in those specific life areas. As you read through this section, pay specific attention to which house your Black Moon Lilith is in to dive deeper into more about how her archetype shows up in your life.

Black Moon Lilith in the first house and the ascendant is covered in depth in Chapter 3; we'll go into the rest of the houses here.

BLACK MOON LILITH IN THE SECOND HOUSE

The second house in astrology is ruled by the zodiac sign Taurus and planet Venus, representing possessions, ownership, talent, material resources, earned income, finances, security, stability, the physical senses, worth, the earthly realm, self-esteem, and one's personal values. This area of your chart indicates your monetizable gifts and how you can create material wealth for yourself. When Black Moon Lilith is here, you can experience power struggles, loss, or obstacles around your money and material resources. The energy can flow from one extreme to the other: either you grew up in poverty, and this drives you to ensure your financial security; or you can experience a difficult loss of resources.

You are also an innovative and rebellious free spirit when it comes to monetizing your talents and gifts. Entrepreneurialism, radical ways of obtaining material resources, or transformative financial ideas can be your superpowers, but only if you can release the shadows of low self-worth, lack, and fear from past traumas. Steve Jobs had Black Moon Lilith in Scorpio in his second house, and you can see a breakdown and a rise from the ashes in his work and how he made a living. He was fired from Apple Inc. in the mid-1980s because, with his harsh demeanor, he was deemed difficult to work with. In men, Black Moon Lilith can bring out more of the Adam archetype of unintegrated dark masculine control, dominance, and aggression. When Jobs was brought back as CEO of Apple in 1997, he completely turned the brand around and revolutionized the digital media, music, and tech world with launches of groundbreaking products like the iMac and iPod. Essentially, his dark masculine had to be integrated before he was able to turn his vision around.

Black Moon Lilith also represents raw sexual magnetism and primal emotions. You can monetize your look or aesthetic, triggering criticism from the patriarchy or breaking old, traditional beauty standards. You may equate your sexuality with your self-worth and what you have of value to offer to others. You may use this dark, divine feminine energy force to attract material gains into your life. Bettie Page, an iconic 1950s pinup and bondage model, had her sun and Mercury in Taurus, and Black Moon Lilith in Taurus in her second house, forming an opposition with expansive Jupiter retrograde in seductive Scorpio in the eighth house of sex. We will dive into what an opposition is in Chapter 6.

She was tragically a victim of a tumultuous childhood in poverty and suffered sexual trauma from men, including her own father, throughout her life. She created a living for herself posing for and selling her nude photographs to thousands of admirers. The photos of her scantily clad figure were considered so taboo for their time that she triggered an investigation by the FBI, who villain-ized her feminine sexuality. It's rumored that even those investigating her had subscriptions to her pinup photos on the down-low. After the investigation, she became a recluse and turned to evangelical Christianity. She passed in 2008, but she is still known and revered as the Queen of Pinups and an icon of feminine power and sexual free-dom. Unfortunately, Page died penniless, but her brand still generates material wealth through the licensing of merchandise like retro-inspired lingerie, clothing, shoes, and accessories.

You also can experience financial loss, and through this destruction of your stability, you gain the wisdom and self-empowerment to change it. There also can be power struggles over money, placing a strain on romantic and personal relationships. A beloved client of mine, Mara, has experienced upheaval, transformation, uncertainty, and challenges around her finances throughout her life. Her Black Moon Lilith is in exaltation in the dark sign of Scor-pio in her second house. In her sessions, she essentially had to go through deep alchemy and face the shadows of what is holding back abundance in her life. Low self-worth and believing that she is not enough is a major theme in regard to this.

Prince Harry, Duke of Sussex, is a public figure with Black Moon Lilith in the independent sign of Aries in his second house. This manifested when he left the monar-chy with his wife Megan Markle, the Duchess of Sussex, on January 8, 2020, and as a result was cut off from any of his family's financial benefits. It's important to add that this time was his fourth Black Moon Lilith return at age 36 (turn to Chapter 6 for more on this rebellious life cycle event). He broke away and became fiscally independent; he and his wife have become savvy at creating their own wealth through television specials, interviews, and his controversial memoir, *Spare,* which was published in 2023. His Black Moon Lilith in Aries is forming a challenging connection to his natal Jupiter in Capricorn in his twelfth house of endings and exile, amplifying his loss of wealth. Jupiter represents growth, luck, and wealth, but Prince Harry's is in its *fall* (unfortunate) in Capricorn, which can represent restriction or delays before prosperity can occur. Also, the year this took place, there were life-changing eclipses activating Capricorn and Cancer: in his first and seventh house representing his identity and his marriage partner. This was at the time of his Jupiter return, a burst of luck that occurs every 12 years, activating both the loss of his royal money and the gain of his and his wife's sovereignty plus lucrative financial independence. This breaking away echoed the actions of Lilith in her archetype. On top of it, the media dubbed the couple's departure "Megxit," a misogynistic slur that reminds us of the negative energy Lilith experienced in her mythology from Adam.

BLACK MOON LILITH IN THE
THIRD HOUSE

When Black Moon Lilith is placed in your third house, your voice triggers transformation in others through radical authenticity and rebellion. The third house in astrology is ruled by the wordsmith zodiac sign Gemini and celestial mental magician Mercury. This area of the chart represents one's intelligence, writing, the voice, singing, communication, and how you express your thoughts to the world. When Black Moon Lilith is in this area of your chart, your thoughts, ideas, and verbal expression can go against societal norms, for which you face the risk of rejection or demonization at first. Your words can spark conflict; they can be a source of self-empowerment for some, yet trigger uncomfortable transformation in others. You break with tradition and channel your traumas through your vocal expression to impact and transform the world.

In this situation, your voice is a tremendous gift, but the outside world blocks you from speaking your truth until later in life. Your voice also can heal others. Maya Angelou is a notable African American author, poet, singer, and dancer. She is a Black Moon Lilith in Scorpio, in the third house, who channeled her childhood trauma into her voice and self-expression in one of her greatest works: *I Know Why the Caged Bird Sings*. In this book, she details her childhood from ages 3 to 16 and includes heavy themes of rape, misogyny, and racism—all are events, unfortunately, that are in alignment with the energy of Black Moon Lilith in the sign of Scorpio. In it, the trauma she experiences renders her unable to speak for several years afterward. Angelou's entire career was to share the lens of the Black women in America to heal others through the written word.

In the modern day, the third house has also played more of an integral role in people's everyday lives due to the rise of social media, marketing, e-mail, texting, and the online revolution. Papers, documents, contracts, and letters also are facets of life situated in the third house. Consider again Britney Spears (mentioned in Chapter 4), who is a freedom-loving Sagittarius sun with contractual Mercury, Black Moon Lilith, and illusory Neptune in the third house. On top of the controlling public conservatorship battle with her family, she also has dealt with bullying from the media and paparazzi about her life.

The third house also represents siblings in addition to social media and the press. Kendall Jenner is a media personality and model whose siblings and entire family became famous with the help of reality TV, blogs, social media channels like Instagram, and the press. The public has a polarized relationship with the Kardashian-Jenner clan, and this is exemplified with Kendall's Black Moon Lilith in Gemini, centered in the third house.

BLACK MOON LILITH IN THE FOURTH HOUSE

The fourth house represents one's emotional core, home environment, roots, family, parents, and ancestry. The emotional water sign Cancer and the maternal moon both rule over and are comfortable in this house. Since Black Moon Lilith is the antithesis of this nurturing lunar energy, it's a difficult and uncomfortable house for Black Moon Lilith to be in. The fourth house is also an angular house, because the cusp of the fourth house is an important angle. This is called the *imum coeli* (IC), meaning "bottom of the sky" in Latin. It also is directly opposite from the career-driven and public-facing midheaven (associated with the tenth house of career), which is also called *medium coeli* (MC), "middle of the sky" in Latin. When Black Moon Lilith is placed in angular houses, it gives more power to her archetype in your life. If Black Moon Lilith is placed in proximity (within 10°) of the IC, it intensifies Lilith's dark energy and influence in this private area of your life even more.

When your emotional core is disrupted by trauma in childhood, family, or ancestral patterns, it creates deeper subconscious patterns that can feel challenging to break away from. Some who have this placement in their charts can experience mental illness, power struggles, lack of stability, emotional turmoil, or abuse in their family and home life. When your foundation is shattered, especially through difficult childhood or ancestral traumas, it can make it a challenge to heal in adulthood. Black Moon Lilith in the fourth house also indicates ancestral trauma, or curses passed down through lineage that negatively affect the members of a person's family. A controlling mother or father also can manifest with Black Moon Lilith here, leading to emotional distance.

Take legendary African American singer and civil rights activist Nina Simone, who was born February 21, 1933 and named Eunice Kathleen Waymon. Simone, who gained popularity in the 1950s and 1960s, was a creative Pisces sun and stern and rebellious Aquarius ascendant with Black Moon Lilith Gemini influencing her fourth house of emotions, lineage, and family. She grew up poor in the South and, as such, had to endure racism. But as a talented piano player, she broke through socioeconomic barriers by working up through the ranks in prestigious music schools like Juilliard. Because of a rejection from the prestigious music conservatory Curtis Institute of Music, she started playing in clubs in Atlantic City, New Jersey. That's also where she created her stage name to hide the gig from her religious mother. Known for her deep, soulful, and raspy voice, Simone also suffered from mood swings and an angry temper. She was later diagnosed in the mid-80s with bipolar disorder and schizophrenia. Her daughter, Lisa Simone, has publicly discussed the verbal and physical abuse she suffered from her mother in her childhood. There was also discord and domestic violence in the home between her mother and father.

For some with this placement, a lineage of rebellion against oppression or power can emerge, as with rebellious activist Angela Davis. Born in 1944 in Birmingham, Alabama, she was in the hotbed of the Jim Crow South and violence from white-supremacist hate group the Ku Klux Klan. Davis is a humanitarian Aquarius moon and sun in her tenth house of life path, with Black Moon Lilith in Leo in opposition in her fourth house. Her Black Moon Lilith is also forming an exact connection with creative genius Jupiter, the karmic north node, and transformative Pluto all in the expressively bold sign of Leo; these amplify her life's role to channel rebellion into her writing and creativity. She witnessed racial violence and the resulting activism by powerfully rebellious women from a young age in her hometown, which laid the foundation for her own activism work later in life. Her mother was also a Black civil rights activist during a time when it was dangerous to be outspoken about racial inequality in the South.

In men, having Black Moon Lilith in the fourth house can also create difficulties within the family unit, especially with the mother, leading to destructive emotional patterns in relationships later in life. We can also see this unintegrated dark masculine energy manifest in the famous Sex Pistols guitarist, Sid Vicious, who was born in London, England, to a single mother who abused drugs. His Black Moon Lilith was in Pisces in the fourth house. He is most known for his addiction-fueled relationship with Nancy Spungen, whose life ended tragically in murder. He was accused of the crime but died from a drug overdose before he went to trial. Spungen was also a Pisces sun, which may have brought to the surface the addictive family patterns Vicious experienced with his mother.

BLACK MOON LILITH IN THE FIFTH HOUSE

Play, romance, pleasure, dating, recreational sex, self-expression, entertainment, love affairs, children, fertility, partying, and creativity are all a part of one of the most fun-filled areas of the birth chart: the fifth house. Ruled by the vibrant sun and showstopping fire sign Leo, when Black Moon Lilith is in this house, she can cast a shadow, transcend societal boundaries, incite rebellion, and manifest radical creativity. Overindulgence in fifth-house pleasures can result from having the celestial dark goddess here. Consider Prince, a Grammy Award–winning musical artist and androgynous icon who rose to fame in the 1980s. His Black Moon Lilith is in fiery Aries in his fifth house, with Mars also in Aries close by on the cusp of his fourth and fifth houses. Aries is a Mars-ruled sign, representing divine masculine sexual drive, war, battles, and passion; it also shows Prince's desire to break down masculine gender norms, which he did with his fluid artistic expression, singular style, and how he infused his unique music with themes around raw sexual freedom, love, and desire.

The dark mother or terrible mother archetype of Lilith also manifests itself here. In a version of her mythology, she was considered a harmful demon who killed babies and children, with the ancients wearing amulets to guard against her dangers. Black Moon Lilith can intensify this malefic energy, creating challenges or power struggles in your own childhood, or in the lives of your children. Prince dealt with epilepsy, bullying in school, and domestic violence; he found solace and self-empowerment in his creativity. In his adult life, he experienced more trauma around his own child with his first wife, Mayte Garcia. She detailed what happened in her memoir, *The Most Beautiful: My Life with Prince,* released after his untimely death from overdose in 2016. Their son was born in 1996, tragically with Pfeiffer syndrome, and passed six days after his birth. Shortly after, the couple suffered another miscarriage. Black Moon Lilith in the fifth house can also influence overindulgence in the pleasures of life to distract you from past traumas and difficult emotions. It's important to note that not all fifth-house Black Moon Lilith placements manifest in the same way Prince's did; it depends on which planets are in the energetic mix.

Controversial African American actor Nick Cannon's fertility matters, children, and relationships have also made headlines in the press and on social media. He has an extremely crowded fifth house including his moon, sun, Black Moon Lilith, Saturn, and Pluto in the relationship, beauty, and pleasure-seeking sign of Libra. Together this potent planetary grouping (a *stellium* in astrology) represents a high volume of nontraditional love affairs, fertility concerns, and children. It is well documented in the press that Cannon has had 12 children from six different relationships; first, there were twins with famed singer Mariah Carey, who is a Black Moon Lilith in Gemini. One child from a different relationship devastatingly passed from brain cancer in 2021. Cannon has openly said he does not believe in monogamy, showing the rebellion against traditional relationship roles with his Black Moon Lilith in Libra.

We can also experience the dark goddess in the fifth house through the artistic expression of the late Janis Joplin. She was known for her uniquely soulful voice as the premier white blues vocalist in a traditionally Black musical genre during the 1960s. She also was a symbol of the brewing women's liberation movement in those days because of her eccentric and sexually uninhibited art. Born in Texas, she did not fit in as a child and experienced bullying, which plagued her with insecurities around her talent when she became a rock star. Joplin was a Capricorn sun with her emotional Cancer moon, rebellious Black Moon Lilith, and expansive Jupiter in her fifth house. She was known for her raw emotion and pouring her heart out through her music—aligning with her dark feminine Cancer energy. It was also reported that she indulged in excess alcohol and drugs, an extreme manifestation of Black Moon Lilith in the fifth house, and accidentally died from a heroin overdose at the young age of 27. Not only is 27 the age of the third Black Moon Lilith return, but also the sometimes harsh coming-of-age that occurs during the Saturn return.

BLACK MOON LILITH IN THE SIXTH HOUSE

Work, daily routine, health, healing, wellness, service, duty, and employment are the areas of life activated with your sixth house in astrology. This is the area of the chart ruled by practical and analytical earth sign Virgo and cosmic messenger Mercury. If you are a woman or person of color, you can find yourself having to constantly break through glass ceilings in your workplace and revolutionize outdated hierarchies. On the other hand, men with this placement can experience difficult relationships in early life with women, leading to rejection of feminine authority in the workplace. You also seek to transform and heal the sometimes harmful system of the wellness industry because of your own difficult experiences, challenges, and trauma in this area of your life.

In a life filled with historical firsts as a woman of color in politics, Kamala Harris is, at the time of writing, the 49th vice president of the United States. She is not only the first woman, but also the first Black and Indian woman to hold the role. She is the highest-ranking woman in the history of the American government, ending over two centuries of the white, patriarchal tradition that is deeply embedded in American politics. Regardless of how you view her political platform, this was an extremely hard glass ceiling that Harris broke through when she was elected. Before stepping into this impactful role, she also was the first Black and Indian woman to hold the offices of San Francisco district attorney and California State attorney general, and the second to be a U.S. senator. Harris is a verbally dynamic Gemini rising with a legal-oriented Libra sun. Her Black Moon Lilith is in Sagittarius in her sixth house, showing how her international background and ethnic identity shifted historic barriers and structures set up in her workspaces.

When Black Moon Lilith is influencing this area of your chart, your health, wellness, diet, and how you nourish your body can be affected by difficult yet empowering shadows when alchemized and healed. African American supermodel Tyra Banks is also known for breaking through barriers in the fashion industry as the first Black woman solo on the cover of *Sports Illustrated* in the early 1990s, and then again as the oldest model on the cover later in her career, at age 45. Tyra Banks is a Cancer rising and Sagittarius sun. Her Black Moon Lilith in Capricorn is in her sixth house, and it's also in the same sign as the aesthetic-and-beauty planet, Venus. Banks was also the host of popular reality and talk shows *America's Next Top Model* and *The Tyra Banks Show*. On top of breaking through racial barriers in her work, she is also known for being an outspoken advocate for diversity, body image, and size inclusivity.

She's stated how it was difficult for her in her early modeling days as a teenager with being called too big or too thin, and having her weight being under constant scrutiny throughout her career. Her experience as a body-positive role model is detailed in a memoir co-written with her mother: *Perfect Is Boring*. After a tabloid body-shamed Banks in 2007 for gaining post-modeling weight in a paparazzi beach photo, she stood up for herself and called out the body-shaming while wearing the same swimsuit on *The Tyra Banks Show*. This was a landmark moment for her as a body-image advocate, and it helped fuel an empowering conversation around how we can celebrate our bodies, no matter how they appear.

In 2020, a couple of years after the end of *America's Next Top Model*, there was a resurgence of social media and press backlash against some problematic moments on the show regarding race, body, and sexuality. Banks did end up apologizing via social media and acknowledged that some parts of the show had been questionable. Regardless of this controversy, Tyra Banks has been a rebellious wellness and body-positivity advocate throughout her career.

BLACK MOON LILITH IN THE SEVENTH HOUSE

The seventh house in astrology explains your life partner and what a deep bond looks like for you. Marriage, relationships, and partnerships are extremely important facets of life. This house shows us how you relate to your significant other, or what qualities a future relationship will display. The seventh house is also an important angular house, in opposition from your personal ascendant in the first house of self. The descendant is the angle that begins the seventh house. If Black Moon Lilith is placed in proximity (within 10°) of the descendant, it intensifies Lilith's dark energy and influence in your relationships and collaborations with others even more. Not only is this area of your chart about your other half, but it also describes business collaborations, contracts, and agreements. Your perceived enemies are also an integral shadow aspect of this life. When you have Black Moon Lilith in the seventh house, Lilith and Adam's divine masculine and feminine relationship dynamic play out in your life. Power struggles, jealousy, dominance, and, even more severely, abuse can occur in your relationships when the dark goddess's energy is left unintegrated.

Tina Turner, known as the "Queen of Rock 'n' Roll," was an iconic African American performer who rose to fame with her ex-husband Ike Turner in the 1960s. She was born Anna Mae Bullock in 1939 in rural Tennessee into a difficult childhood, witnessing her father's violence against her mother. Her parents were poor sharecroppers who split up when she was young, leaving her and her sister to be raised by her grandmother. Turner was a creative Leo rising, freedom-loving Sagittarius sun, with Black Moon Lilith in Aquarius retrograde in her seventh house. She met Ike Turner, an up-and-coming musician, when she was a teenager at a music club in the South. They quickly began a musical business collaboration, which led to romance and then marriage in 1962.

Throughout their marriage, they created chart-topping hits, but beneath the surface, Tina was the victim of terrible physical abuse, sexual abuse, and infidelity from Ike on a regular basis. He also was stunting their growth as musicians—and Tina realized that she was the star of the duo. She understood that he had deep-seated insecurities and worked with him out of loyalty. They were married for 16 years, until Tina quite literally escaped Ike's violence and divorced him in 1978. She left after a violent attack with only 36 cents in her pocket. After that, her career soared, and she met a nurturing and supportive lover in 1986 whom she married in 2013. Her story of trauma and empowerment is detailed in her memoirs and a biopic starring Angela Bassett: *What's Love Got to Do with It*. Tina realized her own inner strength and power, and had the courage to escape a terrible situation.

Kurt Cobain, leader of the 1990s grunge band Nirvana, is another notable seventh house Black Moon Lilith. In his case, Black Moon Lilith was in the sign of Aries, forming a harsh connection to his Cancer moon in his tenth house of career. He was a Virgo rising with a Pisces sun, and his musical expression was in alignment with the emotional water energy of his chart—his band's lyrics were filled with angst. While he became successful because of his talent, his marriage to fellow rock artist Courtney Love was a publicly destructive one filled with discord and substance abuse. He tragically died by suicide at 27 years old. It's relevant that mean Black Moon Lilith was transiting in Aries then, marking his second Black Moon Lilith return (flip to Chapter 6 to learn more about this lifecycle event).

Another example of a seventh house Black Moon Lilith is Princess Diana of Wales, whom I mentioned previously. Known as the "People's Princess," she was a beloved icon of grace, poise, beauty, and humanitarianism. Diana was a nurturing Cancer sun with communication planet Mercury and rebellious Black Moon Lilith in Cancer retrograde in the seventh house. Born in Sandringham, England, in 1961, she saw her parents' troubled marriage end in divorce when she was a child, creating an ancestral relationship pattern that manifested in her adult life. Diana married into the royal family through then Prince Charles in 1981, when she was 20 and he was 32, but eventually the relationship unraveled in tremendous difficulty. She dealt with postpartum depression, eating disorders, low self-esteem, and the relentless paparazzi. Both members of the couple engaged in affairs as the sad and tumultuous marriage fell apart. According to Diana in her tell-all interview with journalist Martin Bashir, Charles was also quite jealous of the public's love for Diana. The marriage ended in divorce in 1996 due to these power struggles.

BLACK MOON LILITH IN THE
EIGHTH HOUSE

Life takes a darker tone as we move into the eighth house of the astrological chart. Sexuality, procreation, death, transformation, the occult, magic, joint resources, debts, taxes, and inheritances all are in this intense house. The dark feminine zodiac sign Scorpio and malefic planets Mars and Pluto rule over this house. When Black Moon Lilith is here, her dark goddess energy intensifies and is in her comfort zone. You can undergo massive alchemy, upheaval, and internal transformation in your life, learning lessons through harsh realities. In some tragic cases, Black Moon Lilith can indicate sexual abuse and trauma. On the other hand, using sex magic or your sexual magnetism is a more empowering theme of this house. Dark creativity through themes like mystery, murder, or hidden secrets can also manifest with the dark goddess in this area of your life.

Agatha Christie was a British crime, detective, and murder-mystery novelist and playwright born in Torquay, England, in 1890. She is the best-selling novelist of all time, with her books having sold more than 2 billion copies worldwide, and she broke down gender barriers in publishing at a time when women had little to no rights. She was educated at home by her mother and a governess, as girls were not entitled in those days to receive public education. She spent a lot of her childhood reading alone and playing with imaginary characters, which fostered her tremendous imagination. The author of *And Then There Were None, Murder on the Orient Express,* and many other books, Christie was a Black Moon Lilith in the creative sign of

Leo in her eighth house, with the writing prowess of her Libra moon, Mercury, and transcendent Uranus in Libra in the ninth house of publishing. What links her work to the eighth house is the taboo, dark suspense, death, and hidden energy of her genres. It also relates to her becoming a success in the literary world despite gender discrimination. Inheritances are also an important pillar of the eighth house, and this can be seen with Christie as her books continue to sell and provide generational wealth and security to her family.

Sex and sexuality are a major part of the eighth house, and Black Moon Lilith can make this a central theme in your life. You can see this expressed in the beautiful bombshell Sophia Loren. Like Agatha Christie, she is an eighth house Black Moon Lilith in Leo placement. She also has sexual showstopper Mars in Leo close by on the cusp of her eighth house, which influences the seventh house of marriage. This can be seen in her sex appeal on screen; she also creatively collaborated with her film producer husband, Carlo Ponti. Born in 1934 in Rome, Italy, she rose from poverty to being recognized as Italy's most beautiful woman and most famous movie star in the 1950s and 1960s. Sophia Loren is Capricorn rising with her Virgo sun, love goddess Venus, and dreamy Neptune also in Virgo in the eighth house, with pulsating Black Moon Lilith in Leo trailing close behind.

Whitney Houston was a bright star, but she also dealt with a lot of darkness in her life. She was a Pisces rising and vibrant Leo sun with Black Moon Lilith in the relationship sign of Libra in her eighth house. Her career took off in the 1980s, and she was known for her high singing range and strong, powerhouse vocals. Through the years, she had a plethora of pop hits, but she went down the destructive path of drug and substance addiction with her husband, Bobby Brown. She unfortunately succumbed to addiction with her tragic death in 2012.

BLACK MOON LILITH IN THE NINTH HOUSE

Ruled by lucky and expansive Jupiter and the zodiac sign Sagittarius, the ninth house is where we step into wisdom and spiritual growth. The ninth house is an auspicious one, representing the law, publishing, international travel, higher learning, prophecy, spirituality, and religion. When Black Moon Lilith is in this house, your path is to shake up the collective consciousness in regard to all these facets of life with your voice and presence. To gain wisdom, you must experience life and heal others through the expansion you gain. You also can be someone who is persecuted for your spirituality and religious beliefs. Ninth house Black Moon Lilith is here to transform the collective through a message of change.

Martin Luther King, Jr., whom we've mentioned before, is a notable Capricorn sun close to his midheaven, with Black Moon Lilith in the ninth house. When the dark goddess is close to a personal planet like the sun, her archetype is amplified even more in the person's life. Capricorn represents old structure, tradition, and hierarchy. Remember, he was also a pastor, which is representative of a ninth-house life path. His speeches, like his famous "I Have a Dream," would move, mobilize, and activate the collective. Dreams, prophecies, and visions are important parts of this area of life, and his was rebellious, especially during a time where the United States was steeped in racist control structures.

The ninth house also represents the judicial system and government. Margaret Thatcher, conservative former prime minister of the United Kingdom, was a Black Moon Lilith in Cancer in the ninth house. Born a law-oriented Libra sun on October 13, 1925, she was a Scorpio ascendant, and Leo moon. Also called the "Iron Lady," she was the first woman to serve as a prime minister in Europe and Britain's longest continuously serving prime minister. It's interesting that her Black Moon Lilith is in its detriment in the sign of Cancer, a zodiac sign typically representing the home, nurturing, maternal energy, and the relationship with the mother. While Thatcher was a female political figure, she also is the antithesis of maternal Cancer energy through preserving patriarchal values, interests, and dominance, like the former queen of England. Cancer also rules tradition, and Thatcher stepped outside of the typical role of a woman confined to nurturer or mother. She was criticized during her tenure for cutting a school milk program for children, later stating that she regretted it. She was a wife and mother, but her main priority was the country that she served and upholding its interests. Her official biographer, Charles Moore, has stated that she wished she had given her twins more time and attention, believing that she'd failed them.

Publishing and spreading a message to the masses are activated in the ninth house. You can see this in the life of Oprah Winfrey, an African American media mogul who is also a self-made billionaire. Media is a field dominated by the white patriarchy, and Winfrey rebelled and beat the odds of the system. Born in 1954, she is the embodiment of the dark divine feminine, having risen from a terrible childhood in poverty to being one of the richest Black women in the world. Oprah is a late-degree (29°) Sagittarius rising. She is a rebellious humanitarian goddess with her Aquarius sun, Mercury and Venus in Aquarius in the second house of money, forming an empowering connection with her Black Moon Lilith in Libra in her ninth house. *The Oprah Winfrey Show* aired in the 1980s, making its star a household name and laying the groundwork for the empire she has today. Not only does she empower women, but she also incorporates self-help, healing, diverse stories, and transformative movements in her brand.

BLACK MOON LILITH IN THE
TENTH HOUSE

The tenth house in astrology represents your career, life path, how the public views you, and your social standing and reputation. This area of the chart represents when you've learned lessons and gained wisdom and maturity after the ascension you experience in the ninth house. The planet Saturn and zodiac sign Capricorn are the rulers of the tenth house. Some astrologers identify this house as representing the father or patriarchal lineage, while others interpret it as maternal energy, the mother, and matriarchal lineage. This is also an angular house like the first, fourth, and seventh houses and is associated with the midheaven, or *medium coeli* (MC). Planets or placements in the angular houses tend to be quite strong, so you can experience Lilith's archetype more heavily in your career and life path if she's in this house. If Black Moon Lilith is placed in proximity (within 10°) of the MC, this intensifies Lilith's dark energy and influence in this public area of your life even more.

Dorothy Dandridge was an actor and model who rose to quiet fame in the 1940s and 1950s as one of the few Black performers to gain mainstream exposure during Hollywood's golden age. In a time of rampant racism in the United States prior to the civil rights movement, she paved the way for Black actresses—she received an Oscar nomination for Best Actress for her role in *Carmen Jones*. At that time, most Black actors and actresses had to play stereotypical and typecast roles like the butler, servant, "sassy mammy," sharecropper, or criminal. They were not recognized with multi-dimensional characters and were as such completely overlooked by the industry. This reflects Lilith's energy of being left in the dark, demonized, and oppressed. It took Hollywood 72 more years to recognize a Black actress with the Academy Award for Best Actress: Halle Berry, for her role in *Monster's Ball* in 2001. Interestingly enough, Berry also was the actress who played Dorothy Dandridge in her biopic *Introducing Dorothy Dandridge*, in 1999. Even after this breakthrough, no other Black woman has won this award.

Dorothy Dandridge's Black Moon Lilith in Aries forms a close conjunction with her midheaven in the tenth house, amplifying Lilith's archetype in her career and relationship with her mother. Dorothy Dandridge was also a Leo rising, Scorpio sun, and Cancer moon. She had a harsh upbringing by a single mother who also was trying to make it in Hollywood. As a result, she grew up fast and started performing as a child with her sister to make money for the family. Both scenarios are common with Black Moon Lilith in Aries placements; you must be independent and rely on yourself for support. Just like Black Moon Lilith Rising Marilyn Monroe, Dorothy Dandridge also had the dreamy planet of Hollywood, Neptune, in Leo close to her ascendant. However, she still had trouble landing roles and dealt with the frustration and low self-esteem over not being able to live out her life purpose due to racism. Unfortunately, her name has faded into obscurity.

Another iconic African American actor and singer, Eartha Kitt, received mainstream exposure, but her career was unfairly overshadowed by her rebellious political stance. Eartha Kitt was another vibrant Black Moon Lilith in the tenth house, but in the mercurial earth sign of Virgo. She is a Sagittarius rising, Capricorn sun, and Cancer moon. She was born in 1927 in rural South Carolina. Raised in Harlem, she was an orphan abandoned by her parents. She was told her mother was Black and Cherokee, and she was the illegitimate child of the son of a plantation owner. In an interview, she said, "Except for, thank goodness, that the public adopted me." She rose to prominence after her difficult childhood for her hit sultry songs and was cast as Catwoman in *Batman* in 1967, earning her a femme-fatale, sex-kitten image.

She also was an activist who wanted to use her platform to effect change, reminiscent of the rebellious dark feminine energy of Lilith's archetype. Eartha Kitt was shunned after she publicly criticized the Vietnam War at a 1968 White House luncheon in the presence of the first lady, Lady Bird Johnson. Her career in the United States came to a halt after this incident, but then it recovered in the 1970s after she had been subjected to U.S. Secret Service surveillance. Kitt continued to entertain and perform after this career upset. She was able to harness and empower her life with her sovereignty and truth and survived the crisis involved with Black Moon Lilith in this area of her life until her passing in 2008.

BLACK MOON LILITH IN THE ELEVENTH HOUSE

Known as the house of friendship, the eleventh house is how you relate to humanity, the collective, and your network around you. Large groups, your friends, and professional associations also live in this astrological house. This is also the area of the chart for stepchildren, foster children, and adopted children. The eleventh house is ruled by innovative and quirky fixed air sign Aquarius and planets Saturn and Uranus. Fortune, prosperity, and large windfalls of money are another major part of this house. In our friends and associates, we can find the connections and opportunities to create abundance in our lives. The eleventh house is also the place of charity, humanitarianism, hopes, dreams, and your wishes. When Black Moon Lilith is present in this area of your life, you take on the role of activator, black sheep, and rebellious voice for the collective. You may trigger or inspire others with your rebellious perspective, idea, or presence. Experiencing shaming and demonization for your sexuality from your community, large groups, or society can also manifest if you have Black Moon Lilith in this area of your chart.

Eleanor Roosevelt was the longest-serving American first lady, from 1933 to 1945 during the four terms her husband, Franklin Delano Roosevelt, served as the 32nd U.S. president. She was a humanitarian and diplomat, and she was known for her liberal views on race equality, which was rare for her time. Born in New York City in 1884, she was a Sagittarius rising, Libra sun, and Cancer moon. She was extremely powerful and admired, with driven Mars at home with Black Moon Lilith in Scorpio in her eleventh house. While she grew up wealthy, her family valued community service. Eleanor Roosevelt's dark feminine energy in her eleventh house came through in her philanthropic actions and activism work while she was in the White House. In 1939, she famously quit the Daughters of the American Revolution (DAR) because they wouldn't let legendary African American opera singer Marian Anderson perform at Constitution Hall, a DAR venue near the White House. She also served as a delegate to the United Nations after her husband passed, helping to draft the Universal Declaration of Human Rights.

Having Black Moon Lilith in the eleventh house can also put your sexuality on display for the collective. Demonization or shaming of it can take place, also channeling the archetypal energy of Lilith. Pamela Anderson is a public figure who dealt with the leaking of her private home videos to the public. She was a small-town girl born in Canada in 1967 and became famous for posing in *Playboy*, her role in *Baywatch* in the 1990s, and her marriage to Mötley Crüe drummer Tommy Lee. They married within four days of meeting in 1995. She is a Gemini rising, Cancer sun, with an Aries moon. Her dark feminine energy is powerfully amplified with her Aries moon, Black

Moon Lilith, and Saturn in her eleventh house. You also can see this exemplified in Anderson's career as a model, actor, and modern-day pinup. However, when the private tape between her and her then husband was leaked, it was Anderson who faced judgment and shaming from society. The situation showed how sexist our patriarchal society and the entertainment industry is.

Anderson also has a polarizing effect on the public; she receives either love or hate, with nothing in between. In the spirit of an eleventh-house Black Moon Lilith, we also see her entire life laid out for society to witness—and judge. Not only is Black Moon Lilith in Anderson's eleventh house; she is forming almost an exact connection with the Moon, a personal planet. This gives a harsh potency to Lilith's archetype in their relationship with collective society.

BLACK MOON LILITH IN THE TWELFTH HOUSE

The twelfth house in astrology represents what's beneath the surface, lost, hidden, secret, and secluded. It's ruled by the mutable water sign Pisces, and its planetary rulers are spiritual Jupiter and the planet of illusion, Neptune. This is the end of the line; it's the final house, representative of endings and the unknown experience that awaits us after death. Hidden enemies, your subconscious mind, addictions, prisons, loss, hospitals (and psychiatric hospitals), illusions, quarantines, and the spiritual realm all live in the mystical twelfth house. It also can represent your fears, the dream realm, repression, and ancestral trauma. Black Moon Lilith represents a deep secret fear that you have not faced, keeping you stuck in unconscious patterns in your daily life until you shine a light on them and release them. It also can represent persecution for your beliefs—or this is something your family line has trauma with that became embedded in you.

Lucille Ball was a legendary television sitcom icon with her then husband, Cuban musician Desi Arnaz, in the 1950s. She was a Capricorn rising, with a Leo sun and Capricorn moon. Her Black Moon Lilith was in Sagittarius, tucked away in her twelfth house. This created subconscious shadows and trauma around her freedom, beliefs, and control from the outside world. You can see how her restricted and impoverished childhood created the rocky foundation for the challenging events that occurred later in her life. Born in Jamestown, New York, in 1911, she had a difficult upbringing. Her family was poor, and her father passed from typhoid when she was only three years old, leaving her mother alone and five months pregnant with her brother. Prior to his death, she had to endure a traumatizing quarantine, which created feelings of isolation limiting her freedom. At one point during her childhood, she was sent to live with her grandparents, and while she was there, her grandfather lost everything financially due to a gun accident between Lucille's brother and a young boy next door. This was traumatic for the family, adding yet another layer of loss to her early life.

When CBS came to Ball for a TV deal, she wanted to include her husband. At first, they didn't want to because he was Cuban, believing that audiences wouldn't accept that. Lucy and Desi faced xenophobia at first for their relationship, a theme that can come up with Black Moon Lilith in Sagittarius placements. Eventually the network changed its mind, and his role of Ricky Ricardo broke ground in its day, knocking down a lot of barriers for Latino actors in American television. The pair played a happy couple for the cameras in *I Love Lucy*, but behind the scenes, their relationship was tumultuous. Their *New York Times* divorce announcement in 1960 stated that she was charging him in the case with mental cruelty. She also almost lost her television career during the "Red Scare" in Hollywood, because she had signed up for the Communist Party in 1936 due to pressure from her grandfather. She had to testify but avoided complete ruin. The attempted control over Lucy's beliefs was a challenge for her in her career.

Repressed anger, rebellion, or rage can also develop with Black Moon Lilith in this area of your chart. It's your wild and untamed dark nature that has been left unaddressed and hidden from sight beneath the surface due to shame, trauma in early life, and fear. Because it is hidden, it is only ready to expose itself when triggered or activated. Will Smith, an African American actor, made headlines globally in March 2022 when he slapped comedian Chris Rock in front of a live audience at the Academy Awards. This analysis in no way condones such violence, which was terrible and unwarranted, to say the least. It occurred because of a joke Rock told that was insensitive toward Smith's wife. Will Smith is a charismatic Gemini rising, Libra sun, with an emotionally intense moon and Neptune in Scorpio. His moon and Neptune in his sixth house of work is opposite his Black Moon Lilith in the sign of Taurus in his twelfth house.

Astrologically, Smith's hidden aggression was triggered by the Scorpio-Taurus eclipse cycle that was occurring that same year. The moon's eclipses signal release, reveals, elimination, and culmination, especially when conjunct with Black Moon Lilith and your moon. The twelfth house is also extremely private, so you may only face this shadow head-on during activating events like your Black Moon Lilith return, eclipses, or other important planetary transits (discussed more in-depth in Chapter 6). Your mother also could have suffered severe trauma, abuse, or neglect when she was going through your birthing process or your childhood. You were on your journey from the spiritual realm into the physical, and her trauma imprinted in your subconscious, affecting your reality without you even realizing it. It can be the cause of difficult and challenging events in your daily life. Unpacking your own Black Moon Lilith in the twelfth house brings tremendous ancestral healing and spiritual alchemy if you have this in your chart.

Will Smith came out with a memoir called *Will* the year prior to the famous incident, and in it, he details a shocking and traumatic moment with his father at age nine. It's important to add that this was his first Black Moon Lilith return. He witnessed his father punch his mother, and it followed him for the rest of his life. Around the time of the Oscars violence, he was facing this difficult and dark shadow. This is an example of what can occur with Black Moon Lilith in the twelfth house when men are triggered, although there is no excuse for violence. It's important, if you are the masculine with this placement, to understand and heal childhood or ancestral trauma that could be causing difficulties in your present moment. Smith said in interviews to promote his book that he felt like a coward as a child because he didn't do anything to prevent his father from beating up his mother. While these were isolated incidents, we must remember that when we leave wounds unresolved, they can burst toward the surface in the form of rage to be acknowledged and healed.

$\female$

CHAPTER 6

Black Moon Lilith Aspects in the Natal Chart

ASPECTS IN ASTROLOGY

Aspects are the angles that occur between planets in your natal chart. There are five major aspects in astrology: the conjunction, opposition, trine, sextile, and square. While the 12 houses and the zodiac signs help us understand the where, what, and who in your natal chart, these sacred cosmic connections called "aspects" show us the *how* and *when*. Sometimes called the *Ptolemaic aspects*, they are an important layer in astrological analysis that bring your birth chart to life. Aspects are the energetic language of how planetary bodies connect to and react, facilitate action, and speak with one another. Black Moon Lilith in aspect with other planets shows you how the dark goddess weaves her web of transformation, raw emotion, and rebellion in your life.

Aspects are the icing on the entire cake of your chart, and this information is meant to be layered on after the core knowledge of Black Moon Lilith through the signs and 12 houses. Aspects are classified into two categories: hard and soft. Hard aspects bring change through tension, while soft aspects bring harmony and synergy. When a planet or luminary forms an aspect called a *conjunction* with Black Moon Lilith in your natal chart, it triggers and amplifies Lilith's dark feminine archetype to blend and unite with the other celestial body it's connecting with. A conjunction in astrology is when two or more planets (luminaries, asteroids, angles, and points included) form a connection with one another in the same sign at or around 0°, with an orb of up to 6°. In a conjunction, the two celestial bodies join, taking on each other's characteristics. Conjunctions can be harmonious, but it also depends on the planets involved.

Oppositions (180°) and squares (90°) are hard aspects, and these can provide change, crisis, challenges, resistance, and tension in the natal chart. Hard aspects can bring out some of the dark and difficult side of Black Moon Lilith when occurring in the natal chart. It's important not to fear them, though, because if we did not have crisis and difficulty, we would never change course or make changes in our lives.

Trines (120°) and sextiles (60°) are soft aspects that have a harmonious, positive, lucky, joyful, and easy effect. They make life easier, and they empower, support, and push the planets' energy forward.

Both the light and dark are needed. It's all in how you navigate and alchemize the lead into gold when working with the aspects in your chart. Each planetary aspect between Black Moon Lilith and other celestial bodies has a different effect on your life. Below is a deep analysis of each.

BLACK MOON LILITH AND THE MOON

The moon, also known as a *luminary*, represents your internal soul and your emotional world. It's your unconscious mind, instinctual nature, and the patterns you learned from your environment as a child. The moon also describes the relationship you have with your mother and women in your life. She also rules over the zodiac sign Cancer, a water sign ruling emotions, the home, nurturing, and the mother in astrology. Her orbit is fast, and she changes signs approximately every two and a half days, with her phases waxing and waning in approximately 30-day cycles. She is also a personal planet and is the antithesis of what Lilith's archetype represents, so when the moon forms a conjunction with Black Moon Lilith, Lilith can cast a shadow on this source of inner light, nurturing, and emotional stability. You also can feel cut off or blocked from receiving your most important internal and emotional needs, because that is what you became used to.

A hard aspect, like an opposition between the moon and Black Moon Lilith, can push you to seek external validation if you experienced early childhood crisis or ancestral trauma, or depression or emotional turmoil in your present. These difficult emotions can cause self-limiting patterns that can continue through adulthood until shadow work is done. When a square forms between the moon and Black Moon Lilith, there is also an amplification of Lilith's rebellious behavior, rage, and raw emotion, whether it brews beneath the surface privately or is on display, up front and center, in your personality. This can leave you feeling depleted and unable to create your reality from a space of self-empowerment, bringing in more chaos and difficulty. You also experience a difficult relationship with the mother or family line, may have endured adoption, or may not even have had a mother relationship. You may have been forced to grow up and mature at an early age, having to be responsible for yourself and others. Your mother could have also experienced Lilith's power struggles or abuse in the home. Or she could have been abusive or overly dominant, thus creating a pattern you have of attracting those who also oppress you.

If your moon and Black Moon Lilith are forming positive aspects in your chart, like the trine and sextile, a more empowering manifestation of this conjunction is a tendency toward a matriarchal lineage, or strong women in the family. Your mother was the dominant one, or you may have grown up with a single mother, heightening the maternal influence in your life. Sexual magnetism, rebellion, and standing in your power come after you have shed traumas or crises that have overshadowed your light from early life. Your emotional needs in a serious partnership or marriage require you to have freedom, sovereignty, and a support for your passions in life. At first you may attract people who try to stifle your light or try to control or dominate you until you realize your worth. You also can look for this same quality in marriage, serious commitment, or deep friendship with a woman; femme fatale, dominant, witchy, and magnetic may be your type.

BLACK MOON LILITH AND THE SUN

Your sun is a planet, or luminary, in your natal chart representing your life force, self, ego, and identity. The sun is the only bright star at the center of our solar system, and at the mystical center of your own personal universe. The sun moves through the 12 zodiac signs each year, changing signs every 30 days. The zodiac sign Leo is the ruler of the sun, and they are both masculine; you can also see the nature of the sun in this fire sign representing creativity, self-expression, and leadership. The sun represents the relationship with the father and important male figures in your life. Understanding your sun and the shadows like Black Moon Lilith that block its influence on your life is extremely powerful inner work and alchemy. This is your allegorical gold, life purpose, and how you shine the brightest in this lifetime.

The sun forming a conjunction with Black Moon Lilith can cause you not to experience the stability, support, and vital structure from the paternal figure as a child. As a result of this deficit, there is a wounding with masculinity internally that then reflects in your experiences in the outside world. You feel like you are always going out and *getting*, while never feeling able to rest in your femininity and magnetism. Or on the other hand, if you are naturally more masculine, you feel uncomfortable stepping into this masculinity. This can trigger feelings of aimlessness, pent-up aggression, and lack of drive; this is your body's natural reaction to being out of alignment. This connection between the sun and Black Moon Lilith can delay self-actualization and fulfillment in your adult life until you have released the trauma, fear, or repression around your true self. When we embody our sun, we are living in alignment, which opens the gateway to attracting abundance through the frequency of ease, bliss, and joy.

When your sun is forming a hard aspect like an opposition with Black Moon Lilith, you are meant to transform and transmute what or who outside of yourself is holding you back from the true you. The sun opposite Black Moon Lilith can create delays, backlash, and falls from grace on your life journey toward self-actualization. A cycle of disempowerment can also occur when your sun is forming a square with Black Moon Lilith because of bullying, jealousy, or nonacceptance from others. This can cause you to dim your light at first. Looking outside of yourself to feel whole will end with you feeling depleted. Empowerment comes with understanding that you will always ruffle feathers, and to be authentic to you, you must accept that this is a part of your path. Releasing the opinions of others is also incredibly powerful and is your key to success and inner fulfillment.

When the sun is forming soft aspects like a trine or sextile with Black Moon Lilith, the dark goddess is supporting and helping you to stand in your power. Your presence is meant to transform the collective through your purpose. You shake up and wake up those around you, even unintentionally. You have an easier time empowering yourself and others, and alchemizing opposition into gold. You may have had a father who nurtured or took care of you—versus a mother who worked and was not around as much—shifting your perspective on masculinity.

BLACK MOON LILITH AND MERCURY

Mercury is a fast-moving inner planet, ruling over communication, thought, writing, learning, and how we process information. Analysis, interpretation, speech, and your voice are some of the cerebral facets of the quick-moving planet closest to the sun. It spends around two to three weeks in one sign, and never strays far from the sun. It also has a notorious retrograde cycle three to four times per year that can last up to nine weeks. Mercury retrograde slows down and disrupts the mercurial areas of life like travel and communication. Mercury was the mythical messenger of the gods in ancient Roman mythology, with this same archetype translating into how we interpret the planet's effects in astrology. Mercury's meaning in our everyday lives has also evolved and increased with modern technology and advances in communication, like the Internet. Modern communication like texting, social media direct messages, the media in its current forms, and social networking are ruled by Mercury. It also rules over the zodiac signs Virgo and Gemini.

When Mercury forms a conjunction with Black Moon Lilith, you can destroy, reshape, and build realities around yourself using your voice, communication, and thoughts. Your words can come out raw or harsh at times, but they are at an authentic frequency, ripping off the fake façade that society can wear to distract from the truth of a situation. As a result, you can feel judgment from others around your opinions; or, on the other hand, others can experience internal growth from your perspective if they align with you. Mercury forming a conjunction with Black Moon Lilith can also have the opposite effect; you can trigger others with your opinions and can face persecution at times over what your rebellious message stands for. Writing, singing, poetry, storytelling, or vocal forms of expression can be incredibly healing ways to channel vocal rage and blockages you've experienced in your life.

When Mercury is forming a hard aspect, like an opposition with Black Moon Lilith, difficult events, or challenges early in childhood like bullying or trauma, can also cause you to feel uncomfortable speaking your truth—that is, until you release what occurred for you and heal through your communication or creative voice. There may be opposing opinions or even suppression of your original thought, but it ultimately is transformative for society. Mercury square Black Moon Lilith can make you extremely opinionated, not holding back your truth from others. As a result, others can have polarized opinions of you. Relearning how to step into your authentic and free speech as an adult is common with a hard aspect like a square.

When Mercury is harmonious with Black Moon Lilith and forming a soft aspect like a trine, the written word, stories, or musical topics relating to power struggles, protests, and darker themes in life could be common mediums for you. Public speaking or sharing your message with others is a place of empowerment and liberation. You can feel support for your radical vocal expression. In terms of a sextile, self-expression through words can be extremely soothing, natural, and healing for you, especially if they come from a place of life experience.

BLACK MOON LILITH AND VENUS

Venus is the ancient goddess of relationships, femininity, love, material resources, artistic ability, music, beauty, justice, harmony, and pleasure. Venus rules over the zodiac signs Libra and Taurus and is at home and can flourish in these signs. Like Mercury but a bit slower, Venus remains close to the sun, changing Zodiac signs approximately every three weeks. She also has a retrograde cycle every 18 months, which can extend her stay to around five months. When the divine feminine goddess of beauty, Venus, meets up with the rebellion and destruction of the dark feminine, Lilith, you see intense healing, transformation, challenges, and upheaval in the Venusian areas of your life. Venus classifies as a benefic planet, using her charm, grace, and beauty to attract facets of life like material possessions, money, or a lover to you. But when she forms a conjunction with Black Moon Lilith, there is a difficulty and a rough edge to this goddess planet.

Black Moon Lilith's presence overshadows the opulence, wealth, and abundant relationships that Venus typically can attract into your life. When Venus forms a conjunction with Black Moon Lilith, the latter can cast her dark shadow in the realm of your love relationships. The people you attract can feel karmic, always teaching you to explore and shift down into the depths of your core. Your relationships will always push you to look into the mirror and to change old or self-destructive patterns. You also can have nontraditional views on relationships, especially when it comes to the gender role for a woman. You also can have a dark sense of creativity, opting for macabre, suspenseful, or tragic themes in your work.

Venus is triggered when forming a hard aspect like a square with Black Moon Lilith. You can experience sudden gains and loss of money, financial power struggles, and self-undoing until lessons around your worth are learned and integrated. Jealousy of your appearance can occur, or you can be hyperjudgmental of others' appearances. You also may be jealous and controlling when it comes to your lovers; this can especially manifest in men. When you were a child, you may have watched discord, abuse, or toxicity in your parents' relationship in the home. Or they may not even have had a relationship at all, giving you no solid template early in life for how to navigate this area. As a result, the people you attract in can trigger this trauma within you until you resolve it within yourself first. Money and finances within partnerships, both business and romantic, can be a source of challenge and inequality for you. With an opposition between Venus and Black Moon Lilith, envy from others, jealousy, and competition can be a theme for you. You may stifle your creative light because of this, but the key is to release attachment to others' opinions of how you shine. You may also have to deal with the legal system when it comes to your relationships, finances, and income.

If you have a soft aspect like a trine between your Venus and Black Moon Lilith, you have no problem embracing your raw feminine power and rebellion. This is a potent dark feminine connection, and you can become a champion for women's causes and changing the collective idea of a woman's role. In a man's chart, if he is attracted to women, Venus also represents what and whom he finds attractive—someone self-empowered, sovereign, and with a touch of strength. Or, with this aspect, a masculine partner (if applicable) in your life can be someone who accepts and supports your sovereignty. This person won't try to suppress you like Adam did Lilith in her mythology. You can tap into sex and sexuality to create wealth and an income for yourself. You also surround yourself with powerful feminine people in your life, which helps mentor and inform your own goddess within, especially if you are a woman. If you have a sextile between Venus and Black Moon Lilith, you are able to channel your shadow self into your creative talents, successfully cultivating material resources from it. You also can be someone who passionately fights for the rights and equality of others.

BLACK MOON LILITH AND MARS

Black Moon Lilith can fan the flames of conflict in your life when forming a connection to a planet like Mars in your chart. In ancient Roman mythology, Mars is the divine masculine god of war and has the same archetypal association in Western astrology. Mars is an inner planet spending from two to seven months in each sign, depending on its retrograde cycle every two years. Mars represents masculinity, men, action, drive, aggression, your passion, sex drive, what turns you on, and how you fight or assert yourself. Accidents, surgery, violence, the military, authority, and battles are also sparked by the planet of Mars. Mars rules over the zodiac signs Aries and Scorpio and is also classified as a malefic planet that gives challenging results. When Black Moon Lilith meets with this divine masculine god, they can spark rage, desire, raw passion, and rebellion, symbolic of the power struggles that show up in their mythology.

When Mars forms a conjunction with Black Moon Lilith, the ways that you take action, show aggression, and display passion in your life blend with the conflict of her ancient archetype. Lilith was a dominant female deity who reclaimed her sovereignty against the patriarchal authority of Adam and God, and this is something you feel you must do frequently in your life. If you identify with the feminine, you can experience Lilith's perspective; conversely, if you are heavily masculine, Adam's archetype as oppressor can be a shadow you must investigate and change. Since Mars is a malefic planet, this is a conjunction marked by discord, challenges, and karmic events, which can frequently arise in the area where you have this planetary connection. You also tend to dive deeply and headfirst into your passions, tapping into the frequency of rebellion against society. You can have alternative passions, or rebel against what society deems normal. The shadow of demonization, as well as persecution from others, can follow you, creating conflict in the house and sign where you have this conjunction.

When Mars is forming a hard aspect like an opposition, there can be conflict and battles with others frequently in your life, especially with masculine figures. Your mother and father could have experienced conflict (emotional, physical, or both), creating a pattern of disempowerment in you—especially in adulthood with respect to men. Experiencing violence, crisis, or trauma from the external world is also manifestation of a Mars and Black Moon Lilith opposition. You may also feel like you constantly have to defend yourself from the outside world. With another hard aspect like a square, you also can experience subjugation or oppression by masculine figures in your life. If you are a man with this aspect in your chart, you can have some difficulty specifically with the father figure in your life, which impacts your own masculinity. Your father may also have been in competition with you.

Harmonious aspects between Mars and Black Moon Lilith are a fiery, empowering, and winning combination. While hard aspects can make the aggression and passion of this combination destructive, soft aspects give you success in exuding natural leadership. Mars is the planet of sex and passion, so a trine between Mars and Black Moon Lilith can give you a high sex drive, sexual magnetism, and the ability to attract others. You also can successfully spark revolutions on a micro or macro level and inspire those around you to participate in them. Mars sextile Black Moon Lilith shows that you understand how to integrate the aggressive natures of both, with your ability to successfully obtain your passion. Choosing a job that allows you to motivate and empower others is a powerful move on your career path.

BLACK MOON LILITH AND JUPITER

Jupiter is a slower-moving planet, taking 12 years to pass through the entire zodiac and spending around a year in each sign. Expansion, growth, luck, optimism, higher learning, travel, international matters, spirituality, and a broader perspective all are associated with Jupiter in astrology. Ruling over Sagittarius and Pisces, Jupiter is a benefic planet; therefore, when it encounters other planets, it provides positive results. In ancient mythology, Jupiter was the supreme male god of the Roman pantheon. This is reflected in the meanings of the planet: spiritual growth, and knowledge through experiences, religion, and beliefs. As Jupiter moves through the sky, it influences growth, abundance, and an increase in prosperity.

Jupiter makes life easier and looks out for your highest interest. Black Moon Lilith forming a conjunction to this powerful gas giant increases the influence of Lilith's archetype in your own life. Leaning into your rebellious, raw, and authentic nature is where you will find your cosmic pot of gold and start to experience alignment in your life. You can also exude the qualities of a radical sage: a teacher who takes a rebellious approach. You find fulfillment when you are a mentor, guide, or philanthropist for the outcasts of society or those who are disempowered. You experience the most internal and spiritual healing from traveling to faraway lands. Organized education is not for you, and you seek to expand your mind through life experience versus sitting in a classroom.

Black Moon Lilith forming a hard aspect called a square with Jupiter brings out the shadow side of when you have too much of a good thing: overindulgence, lack of motivation, and inflation. This also can increase the shadow side of Lilith's story, disempowerment, and the suppression she experienced from those around her. We always hear about lottery winners who end up losing it all soon after the windfall. This hard aspect can manifest as seeing a rapid increase in luck only to lose everything or fall on misfortune. While it's easy for you to bring in prosperity and wealth (depending on your Jupiter placement), you also can feel you don't deserve it, making losing it quickly more likely. On the other hand, Black Moon Lilith opposite Jupiter can bring jealousy and distrust of others around your fortune. You can deal with betrayal from others at times because they resent how easily you are able to attain certain things. You can feel judged for what you've created for yourself, and for your talents.

When Black Moon Lilith is forming a positive aspect like a trine with Jupiter, you can experience personal growth and turn the dark energy of Lilith into an opportunity. You can help lead and educate others based on your own life experiences. You experience positive breakthroughs in life when you remain authentic, and sovereign in your ideas; entrepreneurship is another positive trait of this connection. If Black Moon Lilith is forming a sextile with Jupiter, you can accumulate wealth in unique and innovative ways.

BLACK MOON LILITH AND SATURN

Saturn was the limit of the cosmos to ancient astrologers before the discovery of Uranus, Neptune, and Pluto during the 18th through 20th centuries. Saturn is the last visible planet before you transcend reality into the futuristic and spiritual realms of consciousness. In ancient Roman mythology, Saturn was a harsh male god ruling over sowing, seed, and the calendars with an iron sickle. Also representing the concept of patriarchy, he is a dark father archetype, eating his sons out of fear to maintain his power; it was prophesized that one would overthrow him.

Saturn is the planetary ruler of the signs Capricorn and Aquarius, spending around two and a half years in each sign; he takes around 29 years to move through the zodiac. The Saturn return is a notable astrological life cycle that occurs when he returns to the place he was when you were born at around ages 29, 58, and 87. This is where you face Saturn's harsh lessons head-on and experience removal of everything that no longer serves. He represents experiencing limitation, reality, time, structure, paternal energy, authority, and restriction in your life. However, when mastered, Saturn can provide great stability, long-term rewards, and longevity. Saturn also teaches us that time is an illusion and that your limitations are self-imposed; though at times his lessons are severe, through them we break the chains of our reality and expand into higher levels of consciousness.

Black Moon Lilith conjunct with Saturn is considered a challenging connection due to the malefic nature of the planet. When the dark mother meets up with the dark father, you also could have had a cold experience with your parents as a child. Love may not have felt present. Harsh discipline, control, and dominance could have been a theme in your foundational environment. You also could feel like you have an old soul and that you were forced to grow up fast. Saturn represents structure, and Black Moon Lilith's presence encourages you to rebel against society's rules and regulations. Clashes and power struggles with authority in your life can feel draining, but reclaiming your sovereignty is of the utmost importance for you. Being a "late bloomer," or someone who awakens to their power later in life, is another part of a Black Moon Lilith and Saturn conjunction.

A hard aspect like a square between Black Moon Lilith and Saturn is extremely karmic, and it's a challenging aspect to work with in your life. Saturn is classified as a malefic planet in astrology, so his paternal lessons, especially when harshly aspected, can easily turn into abuse and domination from others. The same archetypal power struggle can occur in your life even while the scenarios and people involved may change. You also may experience a toxic relationship with your father with this aspect, creating distrust in the masculine. Or perhaps you have oppressed others, especially women. With Black Moon Lilith opposite Saturn in your natal chart, you can attract the oppressive dynamic between Lilith and Adam with outside forces in your own life.

Saturn's effects on the dark goddess soften when there's a harmonious trine aspect forming between Black Moon Lilith and Saturn. You felt the support and structure from the paternal energy in your life, which encouraged you to step into your true authenticity. You are successfully able to deconstruct and resolve ancestral trauma or patterns that have plagued your family line, especially your father's side. A sextile between Black Moon Lilith and Saturn indicates that there is gold, self-actualization, and a host of possibilities to be found in your hardships and what you've endured in your life.

BLACK MOON LILITH AND URANUS

An eccentric planet, Uranus rules over unexpected surprises, innovation, rebellion, revolution, genius, electricity, humanitarianism, and the collective. Uranus is also known as a higher octave of cerebral planet Mercury. It's a slower-moving planet, spending seven years in any one zodiac sign and taking 84 years to move through an entire cycle. It's also the planetary ruler of the zodiac sign Aquarius. Uranus's role is to break down and disrupt old structures and systems, replacing them with the new. Uranus is like a cosmic awakener and jolt of electricity, shaking you up through shocking events and sudden changes, and completely breaking down barriers in your reality. When Black Moon Lilith aspects Uranus, your independence is of the utmost importance, and you are meant to shake up and transform others through your radical perspective.

Both Black Moon Lilith and Uranus are rebellious archetypes in their own ways, yet both focus on sovereignty and liberation; when they come together and form a conjunction, you are not one to be tamed. Protesting, philanthropy, and championing for the rights of others can come naturally to you. You also take an inventive and ingenious approach to your life, opting for an alternative lifestyle or unique way of being. An uneventful, humdrum life is not for you.

When Black Moon Lilith is square Uranus, you can go through shocks of transformation, destruction, and rebuilding in your life constantly. The pair can create chaotic energy in your life, and you never feel as if you have stability. This could be from not having structure as a child, so you seek to duplicate this familiar erratic energy in adulthood. Living a nomadic lifestyle could serve you. Black Moon Lilith opposite Uranus represents when others shame or demonize the alternative way that you live or your inventive ideas. You can feel like the outcast or black sheep, only to later realize that you are here to break generational curses and completely shake up the direction of your family line. This is also a "mad scientist" connection, with your focus on intellectual matters and expanding your consciousness—so much so that you take an unemotional and logical approach to life, at times missing out on deeper human affinity.

Black Moon Lilith supporting Uranus with a trine connection indicates that you find your spark of genius when you embody your raw and most authentic self, releasing societal expectations. You have an eccentric point of view that others either love or hate. Black Moon Lilith sextile Uranus also can lead to beneficial life breakthroughs from feminine figures in your life. You also can be a champion and helpful to those who are underserved and unseen in society. You are here to break down old limiting structures and use your gifts to liberate and uplift others. Philanthropy or being dedicated to helping large groups of people can come naturally to you if you have this harmonious aspect in your chart.

BLACK MOON LILITH AND NEPTUNE

In ancient Roman mythology, Neptune is the mythical god of the sea who ruled with his trident staff, which is also the planet's glyph in astrology. He is a ruler of the zodiac sign Pisces, with quite a long orbit of roughly 14 years per zodiac sign and around 165 years in a full cycle. Neptune rules over facets of life like the oceans, glamour, illusion, creativity, addiction, the spiritual realm, and sacrifice. As he moves through the sky and connects with other planets, he can cause dissolution and transcendence of this physical realm. Neptune also rules over the subconscious mind, dreams, and magic.

If Black Moon Lilith is forming soft aspects with Neptune in someone's natal chart, they can rise to prominence in creative fields. It's also highly possible for them to tap into their ability to manifest through magic or esoteric practices. Neptune is considered a higher octave of Venus, with movies, fashion, aesthetics, and entertainment as large factors in its creative light side. Loss, addiction, and escape—the dark side of Hollywood—can plague people who have hard aspects between Black Moon Lilith and Neptune.

Black Moon Lilith conjunct with Neptune is a magnetic and creative but potentially destructive connection, depending on your own unique chart. The key is not to get lost in suffering or addiction to escape reality. Although Neptune is not classified officially as a malefic, when forming a connection to another point or planet, it can dissolve, distort the truth, and create lack of clarity. When Black Moon Lilith is in opposition to Neptune, addiction to substances can be an extreme manifestation of this placement. You also can receive some backlash or even vilification of your spiritual beliefs, experiencing oppression from the outside world. You can experience loss and the dissolution of your reality at various times of your life with this aspect.

When Black Moon Lilith is forming a soft aspect like a trine, you can ooze sex appeal and find successful work in enchanting fields like the arts and entertainment. Others support your creative vision, and you tap into past challenges as a muse for your expression. Black Moon Lilith sextile Neptune allows you to create your own world through the outlet that aligns best for you. When you can channel your traumas and life experiences into artistic endeavors, it's an empowering outlet for you versus seeking escape through people or substances. This could be through any medium that resonates with your soul.

BLACK MOON LILITH AND PLUTO

Pluto is physically small and the farthest away from the sun, but it packs a powerful punch in your natal chart. It takes Pluto roughly 12 to 30 years to move through one zodiac sign and 248 years to cycle through the entire zodiac. Pluto is a slow-moving planet that deals with the generations of humanity at a collective level. In ancient Roman mythology, he is the mythical lord of the underworld, overseeing the dark sides of life like transformation, change, upheaval, crisis, and death.

Like Lilith, Pluto also teaches us the power in transmuting dark energy and learning to surrender. Pluto rules over the transformative and powerful sign of Scorpio, also representing power as well as inherited and hidden wealth, being quietly responsible for the transfers of generational wealth and economic power in governments on a global level. Death, change, crisis, and trauma are some of the most difficult parts of being human, and these are the facets of life that Pluto deals with, making a Black Moon Lilith and Pluto aspect powerful to examine for inner work. Although Pluto is a male deity, he contains dark feminine energy like Black Moon Lilith does, focused on transmuting, destroying, and rebuilding.

It's human nature to have a fear of change, and this is what makes Black Moon Lilith and Pluto a challenging yet powerful pair to navigate when they are conjunct in the sky. You can expect to experience earth-shattering events leading to tremendous personal change. Black Moon Lilith forming an opposition with Pluto in the natal chart can indicate crisis, trauma, and power struggles with authority. What arises could be a pattern from ancestral trauma, past life, or trauma in childhood that causes a distrust of the outside world. Experiencing misogyny or abuse from the masculine also can manifest from square between Black Moon Lilith and Pluto. Clashes with the police or dealing with themes of war can be a part of this hard aspect too.

Dark feminine power is the way to describe Black Moon Lilith trine Pluto. The women in your family may have created its financial breakthroughs, and on occasion, this is an aspect that indicates generational wealth through the mother. You also are extremely magnetic, with the ability to easily attract powerful people who help you on your life journey. With Black Moon Lilith forming a trine to Pluto, you also can have talent in the esoteric and occult arts. You manifest easily with your thoughts, and you can tap into your intuitive power. If you have Black Moon Lilith sextile Pluto, you can monetize your sexuality and magnetism to inspire others.

BLACK MOON LILITH AND THE NODES OF THE MOON

Like Black Moon Lilith, the north and south nodes of the moon are not planetary bodies. They are the two points of intersection between the moon and the sun's path, and they align with the eclipse cycles. These spiritual hot spots in space change signs approximately every 18 months. Vedic astrology explains the meaning of the nodes and eclipses through the tale of a demon named

Rahu. He wanted to become immortal, so he tried to drink the nectar of the gods. As punishment, he was beheaded, and it is his head that darkens the sun during a solar eclipse. The north node is the head of the dragon called Rahu, and the south node is the tail called Ketu.

In your natal chart, the nodes are extremely important points showing your direction and life's purpose. The south node explains past-life talents, skills, traumas, and challenges you've already entered this lifetime with. This is the karmic and malefic side of the nodes: something that must be sacrificed, cut off, or released. Some astrologers also describe this material as what you experienced in your past lives. It represents your comfort zone and your ancestral patterns, and it's easy for you to stay stuck in these old, limiting belief systems. The north node is always in the opposite sign from the south node and is interpreted as your life's direction and your soul purpose. The key is to integrate the skills of your south node and use them to head toward the full expression of your north node, which is the most rewarding energy for you in this lifetime.

When Black Moon Lilith is forming a conjunction with the south node, your family history, past lives, or lineage can have a history of subjugation or persecution. Genocide, war, racism, slavery, witch trials, or other systems of oppression could have affected your family line, leaving you with generational trauma to unpack and heal before you can move toward your purpose. On the other hand, with Black Moon Lilith conjunct to your north node, you can find yourself stuck in patterns of subjugation, oppression, and domination that dim your light and delay you on the path toward your purpose. Black Moon Lilith forming a square aspect with both the north and south nodes of the moon can create delay, internal friction, and upheaval on your path toward your north node. You also can get stuck in loops of self-doubt and disempowerment because of past-life or childhood challenges. Lilith can cast a shadow on your present sacred life journey, creating delays, karmic loops, and roadblocks on the path toward your purpose. You also can feel stifled by others through jealousy and power struggles that cause you to dim your light and not accept who you truly are.

Black Moon Lilith forming a trine aspect with either the north or south node of the moon means that you are here to break generational curses and successfully ascend from old patterns that are no longer serving you. You may have felt disempowered or disrespected, and to deal with this, you isolated yourself to move past these traumas or patterns. While this can feel like a lonely path, in this case, that isolation is necessary. In time, you will find your group of like-minded people as you step into your power and move toward your life purpose. When Black Moon Lilith forms a sextile to either placement, it's your talent in this lifetime to help empower others. You can also break from what your family, community, or society dictates that you should do with your life.

THE BLACK MOON LILITH RETURN

In astrology, the term *planetary return* refers to an event in which a planet returns to the same position in the sky as it was at the time of a person's birth. For example, the most well-known planetary return is the Saturn return, which occurs when the planet Saturn completes one orbit around the sun and returns to the exact degree it occupied in a person's birth chart. Each planet has its own return cycle, and these can have different meanings and effects depending on the planet and the individual's birth chart. The Black Moon Lilith return is approximately every nine years in a person's life—most specifically at ages 9, 18, 27, 36, 45, 54, 63, 72, 81, and so on.

During a planetary return, individuals may experience significant changes or challenges related to the themes of the planet. When Black Moon Lilith returns, you can experience trauma and crisis on one hand, or you can rebel and empower yourself against authority. Any unresolved wounds and feminine shadows can come up, and you will be dealing with the themes around your particular Black Moon Lilith placement. It's not a coincidence that I am launching this book and the *Black Moon Lilith Cosmic Alchemy Oracle Deck* during my own Black Moon Lilith return in Leo at age 36!

Astrologers look to the degree, house, and aspects of Black Moon Lilith in the birth chart to gain further insight into how the return may manifest. As discussed in Chapter 2, it's recommended to use the true Black Moon Lilith since it's a major transit in a birth chart. To begin the healing process around your Black Moon Lilith return, it's important to first know what house and degree Lilith is in your chart. Once you find this, you can calculate the years when you have experienced this transformative life event, noting what you experienced during those times. You can then flip back to the parts of Chapters 4 and 5 that match your Black Moon Lilith house and sign placement and align their interpretations to your return experience.

BLACK MOON LILITH AND ECLIPSES

Observing and recording eclipse cycles is one of the most ancient forms of astrology. Dating back thousands of years as far as to the ancient Babylonians, they were regarded as omens aligning with major societal events like the deaths of kings. In this section, however, we will discuss the effects of eclipses on Black Moon Lilith in the natal chart, not on a collective level. Black Moon Lilith is not the moon, but since her energy is the lunar apogee, I believe eclipses do have a major effect on her energy in your life. They can activate, reveal, and transform the area of life where Black Moon Lilith is in your chart. Some eclipses are more empowering than others; it depends on the type and how it affects your chart.

There are two types of eclipses: solar eclipses, which occur at a new moon when the moon passes between the sun and the earth, and lunar eclipses, which occur at a full moon when the earth passes between the sun and the moon. The difference between a new and full moon and eclipses is that eclipses always occur close to the north and south nodes of the moon (the end of Chapter 8 details more on these astrological points in space). When an eclipse occurs near the north node, it is believed to be a time of growth and forward momentum, and when it occurs near the south node, it is believed to be a time of release and letting go of the past.

Eclipse seasons occur in opposite signs aligned with the nodes of the moon twice a year, but not every one will activate your Black Moon Lilith; you must find the cycle that aligns with your placement. According to my research, eclipse cycles in the same zodiac sign and house as your Lilith placement have the most potent effect.

Paying attention to the yearly eclipse cycles and under-standing which are in the same sign as your Black Moon Lilith are the key to knowing when this is coming up for you. Eclipses won't be hitting your Lilith every single year; they repeat in cycles around every 19 years. You can dis-cover more by looking up the eclipse cycles in an astrology program or ephemeris; align them with your Black Moon Lilith placement.

⚸

CHAPTER 7

Manifesting
with Lilith

We are now moving away from the astrology of
Black Moon Lilith and diving into manifestation and the
alchemical power of your Black Moon Lilith through tapping into your inner sorcerer to manifest with dark energy.
I use astrology for tracking transits and analyzing birth
charts, but it's also an incredibly powerful tool for healing, manifestation, and alchemy. One could say manifestation is a modern way of describing the ancient practice of
alchemy—except alchemy is more about self-actualization
versus just attracting things to you.

We all are magical beings moving with the ebb and flow
of the cosmos. Believe it or not, you are *always* manifesting
and creating your reality. The question is, are you doing
it *consciously*? There are different methods for harnessing
this power—like magic, rituals, the law of attraction, journaling, and affirmations. The foundation that truly amps

up your manifestation practice is pairing knowledge of your astrology with spiritual alchemy wisdom.

YOU ARE AN ALCHEMIST

Part of the practice of alchemy is identifying the lead in your life that's weighing you down and holding you back from who you really are. Unhappiness, internal tension, restriction, traumas, and challenges are symptoms of what's dimming your light. This can manifest in your everyday life like feeling too afraid to share your artistic truth, so you never go after the creative idea you've always had. You could have suffered abuse as a child, or your family line endured trauma and passed it down to you, limiting you as a person in the present. Or you could feel in a perpetual loop of lack around finances, not realizing that it stems from what you grew up with and that you must resolve this feeling within to experience financial breakthroughs.

All of this is tied to how we manifest and create our reality, and dark energy can bring delays and unconscious manifestations into it until we do the shadow work to shift them and turn them into gold. The key to working with your shadow is to love and accept yourself, and not to be afraid of what you find when you go deep. The more you clear and integrate the dark energy of fear, guilt, or shame that can come with your Black Moon Lilith placement, the more pathways open for what is meant for you to manifest through synchronicities into your life. Your astrological chart is a map of shadow work, and understanding dark or challenging placements in your natal chart like Black Moon Lilith is like looking into an honest and empowering mirror. It helps you to understand what—or who—is energetically blocking your way.

Feeling stuck in a rut, or unresolved, self-sabotaging shadows that come out, can destroy opportunities or completely stop them from coming in altogether. Lilith informs us of this dark side so that we can empower ourselves and transform our lives for the better. For example, let's take a common theme I've coached many of my clients on: money and feeling unable to attract it. Yes, practical money management skills are important, but the scarcity mindset is almost always tied back to beliefs, trauma events, or ancestral patterns where there was fear around money—typically, this type of shadow around money is associated with Black Moon Lilith in Taurus or the second house. Money is the energetic currency of this world, so naturally, once you are in alignment with your truth, it will find and be attracted to you.

Not every moment in life is light and rosy, and the dark mother Lilith is there to empower, transform, and do what's best for you when times are tough. She also will rear her ugly head when left untended. Dark gods and goddesses like Lilith, Mars, Saturn, or Pluto have been around since the dawn of time, and your birth chart is the gateway to connect with these ancient deities and empower yourself through their archetypal myths. While their presence can induce fear, this is where the alchemical lead lies in your chart, just waiting for you to turn it into gold like the magical alchemist that you are. Overcoming tragedy, internal transformation, and ascension are all parts of life, and the dark gods and goddesses all are here to support you on that journey.

As noted earlier, you can compare manifestation, setting your intentions, and creating your reality to the ancient practice of alchemy. Linked with astrology, alchemy is not just about turning physical lead into gold; it's an ancient Kemetic (Egyptian) science of soul ascension. It spread to Hermetic Greece and Rome and is now used by modern mystics alongside other esoteric practices like astrology. It's about true self-empowerment and stripping away the societal programming, trauma, and shadows that are not the true you so you can embody your soul's gold: your sun in astrology. Alchemy is not about attracting just material things; it's about embodying your true path and attracting the abundance and support from the universe to do it. It's about releasing the low-vibrational emotions of fear, lack, doubt, shame, guilt, and blame and stepping into true empowerment of self regardless of outside circumstances. It's also about using your privilege and power to aid others on your way upward to ascension.

To manifest with Lilith, look at how she's placed in your natal chart and then read and absorb the interpretation of those placements. Those point to the main blockages in your river of manifestation. Shining a light on what you must change within is the first step to manifestation and alchemy on a soul level. The next is to do the energetic work necessary to integrate the changes into who you are, clearing what no longer serves. This process depends on you. Black Moon Lilith analysis is the foundation and jumping-off point for your manifestation practice, so take time to integrate the interpretations in the early part of the book fully. I've included a shadow-work workbook infused with alchemy in Chapter 9, which I encourage you to incorporate into your daily spiritual practice.

If you place your importance in the things you want to manifest—versus first shifting your energy internally—you can feel frustration and be stuck in a cycle of not manifesting whatever it is you wish, whether it's in the area of love, work, career, finances, family, or self-empowerment. Once I started to create from the inside out, using my astrological chart as a guide to who I am and what my limiting shadows are, it transformed my entire life, and I brought in the life path, partner, home, city, friends, and life that was in alignment with my true self in my birth chart. I first had to understand and heal my dark feminine through my astrology and my spiritual practices, protecting my energy and reclaiming my worth while also identifying who I was and what my talents were. When you love what you do, you can't help but be high vibrational so that you attract and magnetize support.

It's not just about writing intentions, affirming, and believing. Alchemy is about knowing who you are through your astrology, and using the information from the dark energy, like Black Moon Lilith, to clear whatever from your past or even past lives is blocking your progress. It's about coming into alignment with who you are so that the feeling of joy—elation—opens pathways and magnetizes and attracts more opportunities to you. You also release the need to please others or fear your sovereignty, and you rebel for your truth, raising your capabilities, your belief in yourself, and your frequency even more. This all compounds on itself, and that is when you start to manifest money and material wealth through what you are doing—and how you feel while you are doing it. Alchemy is about becoming you—not about what you do, what other people say, or how hard you work. When you decide to create from a space of what aligns with your higher self, manifesting starts to move with ease and grace.

We are all magical beings. In fact, you are *always* creating your reality; the question is whether you do so consciously or allow dark energy to run the show, causing tension and grief. Unfortunately, trauma, challenges, roadblocks, and difficult events can knock us off the path toward who we truly are. There are also systemic reasons like racism, gender inequality, patriarchy, and corporate structures that can delay much of humanity from living out the purpose the universe bestowed upon them. This is the most challenging part of manifestation: the different levels of privilege embedded into this white, patriarchal world. Built-in barriers like classism, racism, and sexism can delay your ability to create and manifest on command. While challenging, it is possible to break through them, and you can see that in the lives of the people mentioned in this book. Your family and society program you from a young age, and their programs wrap themselves around your true DNA, stunting their growth and progress toward your life's purpose. Changing these patterns or shadow aspects of yourself through acknowledging and shining light on them will trigger healing in you on a deep, cellular level.

INTEGRATING YOUR DARK FEMININE AND MASCULINE

Black Moon Lilith is not just an astrological concept; she holds tremendous alchemical information for healing, balancing, and embracing both feminine and masculine energies within you. Masculine and feminine are two polarities and energetic forces in the universe that live in all things. Let's take a step back and consider Lilith's myth once again.

While Lilith in the modern day is seen as a feminist icon (and indeed she is), her myth is also about the shadow side of relationships. She was an empowered female figure, but she also is an allegory of misogyny, of the casting out, oppression, control, and subjugation of women. Adam tends to be a minor character in many interpretations of Lilith's archetype, but in reality, he plays a major role and also can be an "aha" moment for a man's natal chart and his relationship with women. In men, Black Moon Lilith can take on Adam's shadow characteristics if poorly aspected or placed in the natal chart. In a man with an unhealed Black Moon Lilith, there can be wounding or pain from women (potentially a mother) in your life, or you can be the aggressor. Lilith is the feminine wound that has plagued humanity throughout history and from which we only just started to progress in the United States with the women's liberation move-. ment in the mid-20th century. The key to continuing to progress racial, gender, and sexual equality is for the collective to heal its relationship between the feminine and masculine within its members first. To do that, you must know the deepest wounds that live within you so that the healing reverberates out into the collective. Women have been programmed by the patriarchy just as much as men, and now is the time for us to unpack the trauma this has caused the collective. We can do this by understanding the nature of both energies through the laws of the universe and astrology.

Goddess worship is not just for women; it's for men too. Working with goddess energy can improve your relationships with the feminine figures in your life. The empowered dark feminine has healed and ascended from past traumas and self-destructive behaviors, and she can make decisions from an informed space. Old patterns and allowing others to disempower you have been deconstructed and shifted. You have learned lessons from past hardships and set up strong boundaries to protect your space and energy. You're reintegrating your femininity that was once stripped away or lost. You now rest, receive, and magnetize what you want to you versus having to overwork and drain yourself like in the past.

You are able to find a container of stability and support from the masculine and can discern and walk away from men who don't offer this. You trust, but you always listen to your intuitive guidance and navigate your reality from a spiritually informed space. You are releasing the shadows that have held you back from your magnetic feminine power. The empowered dark masculine has released toxic patriarchal templates for masculinity. If this is you, you have integrated wounds from the mother or other feminine figures in your life and now move with the wisdom of your past chaos. You do not try to control the feminine but rather balance with this energy and allow it to create and flourish with safety in your presence.

We can tap into alchemical power in our spiritual practice to heal the dark energy in our natal chart. Astrology is not just about interpreting what will be; it also is about facing ourselves in the mirror and understanding who we truly are, healing from the inside out.

The Hermetic principles are a guide to the universal and significant in alchemy, and they can teach us how to work with and balance these forces of the universe within ourselves to lead happier and more fulfilling lives. This is a cosmic dance that appears inside of you, and learning how to harmonize, heal, and work with both energies is liberating. It's metaphysical law that for a healthy human dynamic, we must balance, honor, and empower both sides of the masculine and feminine polarity within ourselves. If one overpowers the other in the world, it can lead to chaos and imbalance like in Lilith and Adam's relationship. Their myth explains the importance of this ancient energy flow and the terrible consequences for humanity if it's interrupted.

The Hermetic principle of gender states that masculine and feminine energy is found inside of everything and everyone, manifesting on the physical, spiritual, and mental planes. For peace, harmony, and creation to occur, both must be sovereign, and able to exist in freedom, which has not been the case throughout history. This unity of these two energies in humans, plants, animals, places, and things provides a stable foundation for an aligned and harmonious reality. Lilith's plight is allegory for the conflict, turmoil, and misalignment that can occur when this natural balance is disrupted by Adam's need for dominance and Lilith's submission versus a state of collaboration and benevolent masculine leadership. The key isn't to stuff down, vilify, and persecute either the masculine or feminine; it's about understanding how to work with both and achieve our own version of internal balance. Understanding how they move within you is also essential to working with dark energy so that you know whether your feminine or masculine side needs more care and healing.

Astrology also can tell us of the nature of the masculine and feminine polarities and how to understand them in your natal chart as you analyze dark energy like Black Moon Lilith. The feminine signs represent the dark, night, absorption, receptivity, emotion, and creativity. The masculine is the opposite, aligning with the day, light, penetration, activity, and energy. You also can take a look at your Black Moon Lilith, the planets, and placements in your chart, what zodiac sign they are in, and how they are aspected. This will give you an idea of whether you lean more toward a masculine or feminine energetic signature. Fire and air signs are masculine, while earth and water signs are feminine. Fire signs are energetic and active, like Leo, Sagittarius, and Aries; and air signs are cerebral and mental, like Libra, Gemini, and Aquarius. Water is emotional and feeling, like Scorpio, Pisces, and Cancer; and earth is sensorial and reality based, like Taurus, Capricorn, and Virgo. If you have a majority water and have deep feminine energy, you will be able to create a life aligned with this energy signature. You wouldn't put yourself in a fast-paced, noncreative, and cerebral lifestyle if it doesn't align with your polarity. The opposite applies if you are an extraverted and masculine fire sign who thrives on external energy and drive. You can understand more of your dark masculine and feminine attributes by looking at the polarity of the zodiac sign your Black Moon Lilith is placed in.

The sun, Mars, Jupiter, and Saturn are masculine planets in astrology. The moon and Venus are feminine. Mercury is classified as neutral or androgynous and takes on the energy of the zodiac sign it is in. While Uranus, Neptune, and Pluto are male gods, they are modern planets that are not officially classified. As discussed in earlier chapters, Pluto also can unofficially embody the dark feminine. This is another example of the balances between light, dark, masculine, and feminine within your natal chart.

Everyone has different levels of masculine and feminine energy in their natal charts, regardless of gender. Astrology can provide the internal map for us, while alchemy provides the tools for us to balance and heal both masculine and feminine to embody our full selves in this lifetime.

☾

CHAPTER 8

Black Moon Lilith and Black Ancestral Trauma

In this chapter, I will discuss the experience of Black people globally as it relates to the archetypes of Lilith and Adam. My analysis is inspired by my years of astrological research; I noticed that this subject hasn't been addressed in the theological and occult literature currently available on Lilith. Most of the discussion has centered around white feminist ideals or an extremely Eurocentric, patriarchal lens, which I don't believe is truly the depth of the lessons of her story. I encourage you to read this chapter regardless of your ethnic background, because it could still resonate and give you a different perspective even if this has not been your life experience. When we heal the darkest parts of the collective, we transform and change it for everyone. Our experience can also provide a template for your own healing, as we are all one from the same source.

The experience of Black women in the Americas who are the descendants of enslaved Africans closely parallels the oppression, subjugation, and persecution Lilith faced from the patriarchal authorities Adam and God. The United States was created by white patriarchs through the exploitation of these women's ancestors, with laws, a structure, and a religion created to keep them oppressed for generations.

When the enslaved Africans, both men and women, were stolen and trafficked to the Americas, they were stripped of their spiritual beliefs, tribal identities, names, and cultures. Most specifically, the women were completely stripped of their femininity, being forced to labor and toil. The men were revoked of their masculinity and had their families ripped from them, also being forced to labor against their will. They lost their bodily autonomy and were under the control of a white patriarchal system. Tapping into the dark energy of your birth chart with placements like Black Moon Lilith can provide healing for this collective ancestral trauma and help you move forward in your present. It shows you how these ancient traumas can manifest themselves in your current life, giving you a guide to heal it.

Black people currently still endure racism on a global scale, not just in the United States; we can look at racist systems like apartheid in South Africa or oppressive colonialism like the abusive mining and labor systems (which include children) in the Congo. When Black people immigrate to Western nations, they are typically shunned, discriminated against, and looked down upon even though colonialism has destabilized and destroyed the infrastructure of their own nations. Colonialism and white imperialism have destabilized and drained most African countries of resources; these are still reeling in poverty, child labor, and extreme living conditions as a result of it. Extreme poverty, corruption, violence, and negligence of the people by corrupt male leaders is one of the largest challenges in the African diaspora in countries such as Haiti, Congo, and South Sudan.

The *African diaspora* is a term that refers to the dispersion of people of African descent throughout the world, particularly during the transatlantic slave trade. This dispersion has led to a rich diversity of cultural expressions, including music, dance, religion, and spirituality. Members of the African diaspora contain within their very bones the pain and suffering of the slave trade, colonialism, war, poverty, and upheaval of people from the African continent. Lilith's story of suppression and demonization is heavily reflected in their lives and experiences too. If you are a Black person, you are part of a historically oppressed, suppressed, and shunned group; Black Moon Lilith in your chart can indicate the generational trauma, challenges, and wounds that are still present in your life. Lilith rules the old energies that your ancestral lineage had to endure, and these can still play out and harm you in your current life in racist and oppressive ways.

Black Moon Lilith in astrology has a complex and often challenging energy associated with the primal, instinctual, and taboo aspects of femininity. In the context of women in the African diaspora's experience, the energy of Black Moon Lilith can be seen as a powerful tool for reclaiming their voices, their power, and their connection to their ancestral roots. Black women have a unique experience in the diaspora, and Lilith's experience is deeply reflected in their ancestry and current reality across the world. Lilith's pain of feeling unseen, suppressed, demonized, overlooked, and having to rise above a control structure is a common theme, in various ways, for Black women across the world.

On top of the traumatic effects of systemic racism, Black women also endure gender-based violence, misogyny, and discrimination within their own community that tends to be overlooked. Colorism, a deeply ingrained form of discrimination based on skin complexion within ethnic groups, persists within the African diaspora, highlighting the enduring legacy of slavery and colonization. Originating from the brutal system of slavery, colorism perpetuated a hierarchy, favoring those with lighter skin tones and European features over their darker-skinned counterparts of predominantly African heritage. In the context of American slavery, lighter skin tones among enslaved individuals often originated from a combination of factors, primarily the sexual exploitation, rape, and forced relationships between enslaver and enslaved women.

Enslavers, driven by white supremacy, considered these individuals to be closer in appearance to themselves and therefore bestowed certain privileges upon them. This led to a complex social hierarchy based on skin color and ancestry within the enslaved community. Those who possessed lighter skin tones were assigned roles within the plantation household, while their darker-skinned counterparts were relegated to arduous labor in the fields.

Tragically, the ramifications of this oppressive system did not end with the abolition of slavery, and generational trauma persists. As such, colorism continues to shape the experiences of individuals within the African diaspora today. Lighter-skinned individuals often enjoy advantages and privileges denied to those with darker complexions, further perpetuating inequality and division within communities.

Coined in 2010 by author and activist Moya Bailey and seen in social media activism spaces, *misogynoir* is an experience unique to Black women that is now even included in dictionaries and defined as "hatred of women directed toward Black women." The issue also has been discussed widely by journalists and across social media. Based on the word *misogyny*, it expresses how Black women experience both gender discrimination from the male collective, including Black men, and racism from the system of oppression.

Unfortunately, this experience is not over. Most crimes against Black women, and even episodes of police brutality, go unnoticed and unreported by mainstream news and major activist groups in the United States, even as Black women experience the highest homicide rate of any ethnic group in the country, according to the Centers for Disease Control. Atrocities like femicide, rape, and female genital mutilation continue to occur against women by their own people in Africa. The oppression and subjugation of women is a deep-rooted wound in the Black collective that continues to occur in the modern day. Lilith suffered because of Adam's need for control and dominance, and Lilith shows us that this continuing subjugation of the Black feminine will keep the African diaspora in a state of suffering.

While it can feel arduous to think about the layers of ancestral trauma and grief that those in the African diaspora have experienced in the past—and present—we can make a change together to positively affect the future for all of humanity. Lilith is associated with the primal, instinctual, and taboo aspects of femininity, and aligned with the demonization and subjugation that Black women face. Through shadow work with Black Moon Lilith in the natal chart, women of the African diaspora can begin to connect with their ancestral roots and reclaim their power. Shadow work is when we shine a light on and connect to the darkest parts of our psyche. They can use this energy to break free from the limiting beliefs and cultural conditioning that have held them back and to embrace their true nature as powerful and creative beings.

Black Moon Lilith in astrology provides a pathway for members of the African diaspora to tap into their primal power and to reclaim their voices and their place in the world. On top of this astrological shadow work, exploring the cultural and spiritual traditions of the African diaspora and the practices and beliefs of its ancestors, reclaiming bodily autonomy through practices such as dance, music, or ritual, can help you connect with the primal and creative energies of her placement.

Healing ancestral trauma is a complex and challenging process, especially for Black individuals who have inherited generations of trauma and oppression. However, astrology, and in particular the energy of Black Moon Lilith, can be a powerful tool for understanding and healing such trauma. To begin the healing process, it's important to acknowledge the generational trauma that has been passed down through the Black ancestry, which can manifest in various forms, including internalized racism, feelings of unworthiness or powerlessness, and an inability to fully express oneself.

One way to work with Black Moon Lilith in healing ancestral trauma is to explore the ways in which this energy has been suppressed or denied within the ancestral lineage. This might involve looking at family patterns, cultural conditioning, or historical events that have contributed to the trauma. Through deep introspection and spiritual practices such as meditation or ritual, individuals can begin to connect with the energy of Black Moon Lilith and use it to heal ancestral wounds.

Another important aspect of healing ancestral trauma with Black Moon Lilith is to engage in collective healing practices. This might involve participating in community rituals or gatherings, working with healers or spiritual leaders within the community, or engaging in collective action to address systemic issues that perpetuate the trauma.

Ultimately, this healing work requires a deep commitment to self-discovery, healing, and transformation. By acknowledging and embracing the energy of Black Moon Lilith, individuals can begin to unlock the power of the primal and instinctual self and connect with the wisdom and healing of the ancestral lineage.

⚸

CHAPTER 9

Healing with Lilith: 13 Days to Self-Empowerment

Astrology is valuable when interpreted, but the real value comes when the resulting knowledge is absorbed through repetition and integration into your daily life. We've discussed Black Moon Lilith, dark energy, manifestation, and alchemy in previous chapters, and now it's time to put it all together, experience the integration, and take time for reflection.

Ultimately, the goal of this healing workbook is to help you tap into the transformative power of Black Moon Lilith, to integrate her energy into your life, and to use it as a tool for growth and empowerment. There are 13 rituals within this workbook, each to be completed at night. By embracing the shadowy aspects of ourselves and connecting with the powerful, untamed energy of Black Moon

Lilith, we can find healing and wholeness and access our true potential as human beings.

This healing workbook offers a range of practices, meditations, and rituals to help you connect with the energy of Black Moon Lilith, understand its influence in your life, and integrate its transformative power.

Whether you are seeking to heal past traumas, release limiting beliefs, or simply deepen your understanding of yourself and the world around you, this healing workbook on Black Moon Lilith in astrology can be a valuable resource on your journey. By embracing the energy of Black Moon Lilith, you can tap into a source of strength, wisdom, and creativity that has been waiting to be unleashed.

I recommend that you read the entire book before diving into this powerful ritual. I created it out of my courses, workshops, and teachings that were transformative and successful for myself and my clients. You can incorporate the 13-day ritual into your daily life as a continuous practice, or you may complete it as you see fit. Take nights off at any time when you need them for integration and release, and restart when you feel it's comfortable to do so. It will always be here for you to return to when it's aligned.

Each night is designed to help you dive deep into the alchemical magic of your Black Moon Lilith placement through the 12 gates of alchemy and the stages of life represented in the 12 signs of the zodiac. Each day is dedicated to mirror work, a powerful gateway to understanding yourself, followed by time for writing down your raw emotions and thoughts. I encourage you to use your own journal for this, and not to write in this book, so as to preserve it.

Spiritual alchemy, also called Hermeticism, is an ancient occult practice that can be useful for us to tap into in modern times. In alchemy, you are turning spiritual lead into gold through shadow work, self-discovery, life changes, and embodiment of your true and unrestricted self. I've noted that this sacred knowledge dates back thousands of years to ancient Kemet (Egypt); it is said that the Egyptian deity Thoth, called Hermes Trismegistus in ancient Greece, brought down knowledge from the cosmos to help humanity transcend the bondage of this reality. His teachings included things like astrology, alchemy, writing, and magic. He is also linked with the energy of the communication planet, Mercury; he is the messenger of the gods and inventor of writing, knowledge, and information. This is why Mercury, along with Uranus, is recognized as one of the rulers of astrology. Some astrologers attribute its influence to the realm of metaphysical practices.

Translated to modern times, alchemy is the practice of owning your power as the magician, creator, and master of your own reality. The workbook puts this sacred process into practical terms so you can easily integrate the newfound knowledge around Black Moon Lilith. There are 13 parts to this ritual as an ode to the divine feminine goddess. During this process, you will shine a light on your Lilith shadow to empower your life. It is a lifetime practice, and the workbook serves as your guided initiation and introduction to the journey of healing and ascension.

The methodology for this workbook is based around the 12 life stages of the zodiac and the 12 gates of alchemy, with a final day for reflection. Not only this, but 13 is the number of the divine feminine and linked to the yearly cycles of the moon, ruling over motherhood, femininity, and your soul. Doing the work at night is recommended so you can tap into the moonlight right before you head off to sleep. The night is also associated with the dark feminine energy you will be accessing. Each night's session should take no more than 30 to 45 minutes of solitude, journaling, meditation, and affirmations. This process allows the energy of the moonlight and the nocturnal darkness to be present while you access the dark goddess Lilith. On the 13th day, you will look over your journal entries, essentially looking into the mirror of your own subconscious. It's important to be open, honest, and real in your writing during this process.

Materials needed:
A comfortable place with privacy
Cushion or mat
Journal and pen
Mirror (ideally full length)
An open heart

Bonus material:
Black Moon Lilith Cosmic Alchemy Oracle card deck for daily introspective practice.

Each evening before bed, create the groundwork for your ritual by:
Ensuring you have privacy and quiet
Setting up a comfortable spot where you can sit on your cushion or mat
Placing the mirror before you
Creating the ambiance you desire by burning incense, candles, or herbs of your choice
Dimming the light

☽

NIGHT 1:
UNLEASHING THE RAW YOU
WITH CALCINATION

Not only are the 12 zodiac signs personalities or characteristics, but they also explain the circle of life and the evolutionary cycle of consciousness. I've tapped into the power of each zodiac sign to unlock shadows, healing opportunities, and new intentions from those areas of your life with the below thought and journaling exercise.

Aries is the first sign of the zodiac wheel and represents the infant stage when you are first born, and everything is fresh and new. You are more focused on yourself and who you are. This is also the life stage where you are extremely susceptible to the world around you; traumas and ancestral patterns can set in and cloud your true self in adulthood. Today we are going to take time to acknowledge through journaling out what barriers are present in your energy field, holding you back from the authentic *you* that you desire.

Calcination is the first phase of the 12 gates of alchemy. This is the jarring phase of initiation, when you experience a dark night of the soul and are finally able to identify what no longer serves you in your life. You begin breaking up old limiting beliefs, traumas, shame, and fear through the burning down of the ego and what is unnecessary in your life. This is a spark where the shadow of your Black Moon Lilith placement is recognized and acknowledged as a location of healing. Tonight, you will take time to identify and release what is no longer in alignment in your life. This can include thought patterns, people, places, or things that are holding you back from progressing. Use the prompts below to have an honest conversation with yourself and develop the path forward.

At the start of each night's ritual, I want you to do mirror work prior to the journaling prompts.

Spend time looking in the mirror, setting a timer for 10 minutes. There's no need to talk, think, or answer any questions while you do this. Peer into your own eyes and be receptive to what comes through.

Next, answer the journaling prompts below. If anything else comes to you, write it down too. Be honest: write your truth.

Journaling prompts:
1. What self-limiting beliefs are you holding on to that are holding you back from fulfillment?
2. Where do you feel fear and stagnancy in your life?
3. What's holding you back from releasing your fears? What or whom are you afraid of?
4. How can you show up in your life in a more honest way?

Bonus closing oracle spread: After you are done processing and writing each night, you can reflect using your own intuitive guidance with the *Black Moon Lilith Cosmic Alchemy Oracle*. The Alchemy Ascension Spread found in the card deck's guidebook is the perfect way to begin your 13-day journey; each of its cards corresponds with the stages of this workbook. After completing the workbook, feel free to incorporate this same spread daily as needed. The spread and cards will guide you and give you answers to questions that may come up after the workbook is complete.

If you don't have the complementary oracle card deck, you are welcome to use your own favorite tarot or oracle deck. Choose a spread from your card deck's corresponding guidebook that complements what comes up for you. You also can work with a simple three-card spread, interpreting its card positions as representing your past, present, and future.

NIGHT 2:
INCREASING SELF-WORTH
WITH DISSOLUTION

Tonight, we will focus on dissolving what doesn't value you, inspired by the second sign of the zodiac, Taurus. This is the stage in life after infanthood where we thrive on security and stability as adolescents, and we cultivate our self-worth based on our experiences. If this important process is disrupted, it can lead to difficulty in Taurean facets of life in adulthood like money, safety, and security.

In the second gate of alchemy, dissolution is the dissolving of the ashes, bringing rejected parts of the psyche to the surface to be seen, cleansed, and healed. This is when you have finally come to terms with what has been putting a damper on your energy. You are shining a light on your Black Moon Lilith shadow and bringing it to light to be seen to begin the transmutation process.

When you feel unworthy, it creates a dam in the river of abundance all around you. Not feeling like you are able to get out of difficulties like debt, financial loss, not receiving what you deserve from relationships, or feeling drained by others' behavior toward you are all symptoms of low self-worth. It's time for self-empowerment and not to be afraid to shift lack and the feeling of not being enough. Today we will dive into your value, and whether there is any area of your life where you don't feel you receive what you are worth.

Tonight, we shake up and dissolve your reality with the hard question: Where in your life do you accept less than you are worth? What area of life needs attention and clearing? Don't filter yourself—write without fear, so that you can look at the shadow aspects of who or what is coming up for you.

First, set your timer for 10 minutes and complete your 10 minutes of mirror work. This is a time to just observe yourself passively while you look in the mirror.

Next, write what comes through for you using the journaling prompts below. Ensure that you write your raw and real desires, thoughts, and emotions. Don't deny anything that comes through.

Journaling prompts:
1. What part of your shadow are you scared to face?
2. What side of yourself have you left unattended and swept under the rug?
3. In what way do you want to be seen by others in the world?
4. Why are you afraid to ask for more?

Bonus closing oracle spread: Close today's practice with inner reflection from the *Black Moon Lilith Cosmic Alchemy Oracle.* I recommend trying the Cosmic Shadow Astrological Spread. This deep spread allows you to pull in the dark energy of Mars, Saturn, and Pluto—who indicate the difficulties, or lead, in your natal chart.

☿

NIGHT 3:
CLARIFYING YOUR ENERGY
WITH SEPARATION

The zodiac sign of Gemini is the archetype for tonight and whose area of life we are focusing on. Gemini is an air sign representing communication, thought, and mental processes. If we think of the occult symbolism of air as seen in the modern tarot and ancient alchemical texts, it translates to the suit of swords—physical separation, truth, and mental energy. Transitioning from childhood to adulthood as adolescents, we form our social behaviors and awareness of our local community. When we experience trauma like bullying, discrimination, or not feeling accepted by our family, it creates delays and obscures the path toward our true, empowered selves.

This is the stage in life when we develop our speech and thought. The ways in which we think, feel, and speak are how we bring our dreams and intentions down into physical reality as human beings. Without Gemini energy, we would not be able to manifest. This night is dedicated to clearing out the lead of limiting beliefs, fears, doubts, and worries that are holding you back from self-empowerment. This night is also meant for you to separate emotionally from people or energy that are harmful. This is a night to connect with your inner hermit and identify what you should separate with and clear from your life.

Separation is the third gate in alchemy. This is also called a dark night of the soul, where you face your limitations head-on. You become cognizant and aware of what or who is holding you back or creating chaos in your life. In this time of isolation, you can cleanse your mind and think clearly about what is no longer serving you, allowing you to discover your light or true essence of self. This clearing tonight will lighten your energetic load.

First, set your timer for 10 minutes and complete your 10 minutes of daily mirror work. Today I want you to pay attention to any negative self-talk. We'll continue with this focus in the journaling exercise.

Next, write what comes through for you using the journaling prompts below.

Journaling prompts:
1. What are the top five negative phrases or thoughts that came to mind during your mirror work?
2. Why do you believe what you said to be true?
3. Who in your life would agree with you?
4. For each of these people, list five reasons why they are in your life.

Bonus closing oracle spread: Tonight, it would be ideal to use the power of the Black Moon Lilith Dark Alchemy Spread from the *Black Moon Lilith Cosmic Alchemy Oracle*. This will allow you to work through any difficult emotions that come up after your journaling exercise. Turning inward will also allow solutions to come through you.

NIGHT 4:
ACTIVATING YOUR HIGHER SELF
WITH CONJUNCTION

Cancer is the fourth sign and represents the phase in the human life cycle of early adulthood, when we are newly navigating the world—the early years of our 20s. This is a sensitive time, and one where we create our own home, foundation, and security for later in our lives as older adults. Cancer also rules over our emotional needs and intuitive leadership. Tonight, we'll focus on you becoming the emotional leader in your own life. It's also about listening to your emotions as a compass to your higher self and the most aligned reality for you. Leading with your emotions results in an aligned life. When you make decisions from a space of fear, worry, despair, and doubt, your reality will be entirely filled with that heavy energy.

In alchemy, conjunction is the reassembly of the remnants and the rebirth of the true self. You can compare this to the astrological aspect also called a conjunction, where two planets connect in the same sign together and their energy blends. You're finally activating and getting to know your soul's gold in alchemy. This is the version of you stripped free of the limitations, doubts, and fears associated with the lead in your life that was weighing you down.

First, set your timer for 10 minutes and complete your 10 minutes of mirror work. During this session, you can now talk to yourself in the mirror about why you shouldn't do "that thing." You know in your heart what this is.

Discuss the fears, doubts, and reasons why you should not do the things you are holding yourself back from.

Next, write what comes through for you using the journaling prompts below.

Journaling prompts:
1. What or who in your life gives you internal tension, drainage, or difficult emotions?
2. What or who lights you up and fills you with joy?
3. What is the difference between the lists?
4. How can you transform or shed what is giving you negative emotions, and completely fill your life with what's positive?

Bonus closing oracle spread: The moon rules over Cancer, so take in that emotional energy with the Lunar Illumination Spread from the *Black Moon Lilith Cosmic Alchemy Oracle*. This taps into your soul's emotional desires, encouraging you to look at what in your current reality isn't aligned. Release and change aren't easy, and this spread can help you through.

☾

NIGHT 5:
RELEASING THE DARKNESS
WITH PUTREFACTION

The inspiration for tonight's work is the fifth sign of the zodiac, Leo. Leo is the time in life around our first Saturn return in our late 20s, where we are learning lessons about what holds us back from expressing our true selves. Leo represents the stage where we mature and step into our full selves and into the spotlight of our lives. Tonight you will do a final emotional cleanse to remove shadows that keep you away from this magnetic and cosmic spiritual gold.

Putrefaction is the gate in alchemy where our shadow aspects, the ones that are difficult to look at, come up to the surface. This gate forces us to look at those aspects. Scientifically, putrefaction is when something is rotting, and you can allegorically compare this purge to the natural decay process that life requires. Tonight you will identify ways in which you project what you don't want out into the reality around you. Putrefaction is a regeneration process that can feel painful as you acknowledge and cleanse the shadow aspects of your Black Moon Lilith placement.

First, set your timer for 10 minutes and complete your 10 minutes of mirror work. This is a time to just observe yourself passively while you look in the mirror.

Next, write what comes through for you using the journaling prompts below. Again, ensure that you express your raw and real desires, thoughts, and emotions. Don't deny anything that comes through.

Journaling prompts:
1. What was a moment in the recent past when someone, or an event, triggered you negatively?
2. What triggered you the most about it?
3. Does the trigger link to a past trauma?
4. What emotions came up for you when the trigger occurred?

Bonus closing oracle spread: After this emotional session, access the power of the oracle with the Black Moon Lilith Dark Alchemy Spread from the *Black Moon Lilith Cosmic Alchemy Oracle*. Turn inward to find your answers.

☿

NIGHT 6:
SPEEDING UP MANIFESTATIONS
WITH COAGULATION

The sixth night is inspired by the sixth zodiac sign, Virgo. This sign represents when we become seasoned adults in who we are and gain more practical responsibilities. Virgo rules over the realistic and practical duties of life to bring dreams, goals, and ideas into existence. Mercury rules over Virgo, reminding you that if you wish to manifest your dreams, you must set your intentions and put in the practical work to make them a reality. This is the stage in life when we become serious about the future vision of our lives. Tonight's focus is on joining your soul's gold and the energy of your sun with your physical body through the journaling prompts and contemplation.

Coagulation is the sixth phase in alchemy, where you start to naturally embody your true self and align with the attributes, career, and essence of your sun sign. You can tell you are in this phase when you start to manifest faster, and people, places, and opportunities appear in your life at an increased rate through synchronicities. You will take tonight to set your intentions for the future and what you want to create in your own life.

First, set your timer for 10 minutes and complete your 10 minutes of nightly mirror work.

Next, write what comes through for you using the journaling prompts below. As before, ensure that you journal your raw and real desires, thoughts, and emotions. Don't deny anything that comes through.

Journaling prompts:
1. It's time to create from the inside out. What type of life aligns with your soul? Write down five things you want to manifest in your life.
2. Think about your ideal life path or calling. Write down what your day looks like at this work.
3. Now it's time to create your daily life. What does this look like? Are you an entrepreneur? Do you work from home? Are you a leader? What does your family look like? Is there a love partner? Don't hold back! Describe what you want your life to look like.

Bonus closing oracle spread: Since today is about the future and manifestation, channel the power of the As Within, So Without Spread from the *Black Moon Lilith Cosmic Alchemy Oracle*.

NIGHT 7:
UNDERSTANDING YOUR EMOTIONAL POWER WITH CIBATION

The zodiac sign Libra is the inspiration for this night. Libra stands for the time in midlife when you have matured and as such have developed a more expansive perspective of your needs versus the needs of others. Represented by the esoteric symbol of the Scales, this is the balance and equality of both sides of a relationship.

Cibation is the seventh gate in alchemy, when you undergo a purification process through your emotions. It's a time when you are continuously changing and shifting. It includes things like exploring new habits, changing destructive behaviors, and taking action in the direction toward your soul's path. This night is dedicated to making practical changes in your life to make this new you a habitual part of your reality.

First, set your 10-minute timer and complete your nightly mirror work.

Next, write what comes through for you using the journaling prompts below. It's time to create a sense of self-empowerment and contemplate what a balanced relationship looks like for you. These two, combined, will help you create an aligned life.

Journaling prompts:
1. What habits in your life make you feel whole, aligned, and complete?

2. How can you be present and aware of your emotions during your daily life?
3. What type of support do you require from others in your life?
4. In what ways can you give support back?

Bonus closing oracle spread: Adam and Lilith's Relationship Spread from the *Black Moon Lilith Cosmic Alchemy Oracle* relates to the delicate art of balancing who you are and the world around you through relationships. Close tonight's session with a reflective moment with the oracle.

☿

NIGHT 8:
SHEDDING THE LEAD WITH SUBLIMATION

Scorpio rules the shadow, crisis, death, transformation, intuition, and power. Through Scorpio we enter the midlife crisis, or when many of us go through ego deaths and upheaval. This is inescapable for all of us and is an integral part of the cycle of life. This night is dedicated to the transmutation one's soul goes through from the physical to the spiritual. Change is also a part of Scorpio, and tonight you are shifting what should no longer come on this journey with you. This includes things like self-doubt, codependency, insecurity, shame, guilt, and fear. It's time to leave behind old energies, allowing them to die and stay behind in your old reality.

The eighth gate in alchemy is sublimation, the purification process and release of what has been holding you back. The essence of who you truly are meant to embody is all that is left. This is now when you zero in on your intentions and can move about your reality based on what is aligned with you. You'll be like a talented painter who finally receives a break and can then paint in exchange for material resources. You are embodying your gifts and what you want to lend to the collective during this phase and, as a result, you are manifesting the money, things, and people you need to carry out this mission.

First, set your timer for 10 minutes and complete your mirror work. This is a time to just observe yourself passively while you look in the mirror.

Next, write what comes through for you using the journaling prompts below. As always, ensure that you speak your raw and real desires, thoughts, and emotions. Don't deny anything that comes through.

Journaling prompts:
1. What is your purpose in this lifetime?
   (Do not equate this path with money. Instead, craft a path that aligns with what brings you high-frequency emotions, like joy.)
2. What does not support you or encourage this path?
3. How does this lack of support make you feel?
4. Describe the ideal people who support you.

Bonus closing oracle spread: You can complete tonight's session with the *Black Moon Lilith Cosmic Alchemy Oracle*'s Intuitive Oracle Spread. This is now the time to open up to your natural intuition to look into the near future for guidance.

☽

NIGHT 9:
INTEGRATING WISDOM WITH
FERMENTATION

The ninth night's release is inspired by the zodiac sign Sagittarius. Sagittarius is ascended knowledge that you obtain after a midlife crisis, or the new ascended version of you after a death in Scorpio. Tonight, we will discuss lessons, nuggets of wisdom, and how you can move about your life using the past to guide you. Sagittarius is an optimistic energy that looks toward the future as an opportunity versus mulling over the past.

Fermentation is the gate in alchemy where you allow the new life you've created to marinate. You can quite literally relate this to grapes fermenting to make wine. It is rebirth as a fully regenerated spiritual being of light here on earth, using your intuition with ease and creating reality through synchronicities and divine intervention.

First, set your timer for 10 minutes and complete your mirror work.

Next, write what comes through for you using the journaling prompts below. You know now to ensure you express your raw and real desires, thoughts, and emotions. Don't deny anything that comes through.

Journaling prompts:
1. What are the five most important pieces of wisdom you received during the first nine days of this ritual?

2. How can you implement these ideas into your daily life? (Write five practical ways you can integrate what you've experienced so far.)

Bonus closing oracle spread: This is an ideal day for self-reflection with the Lunar Illumination Spread from the *Black Moon Lilith Cosmic Alchemy Oracle*.

NIGHT 10:
AMPLIFYING YOUR FREQUENCY WITH EXALTATION

This night is dedicated to the prestige and power of the senior life cycle represented by Capricorn. Capricorn represents when we have established the foundation of our lives, including the power and prestige we have attained though our calling and life purpose. You can compare this to the wisdom age group of 60 to 70 years old. It also is the archetype of the leader, and when we reach the pinnacle of recognition for our career. Ruled by Saturn, Capricorn can also be the lead of our past, bringing delay and restriction if we do not resolve it. Tonight, through affirmations, you will celebrate and give power to the goals, vision, and light that you want to show to the world.

Exaltation is when you are in the late stages of the alchemical process and you have the feeling of pure bliss from being in true alignment. You can effortlessly create your reality, and you move through life propelled by the light of your soul's path. In astrology, exaltation represents when a planet is comfortable and can thrive in a zodiac sign. You are in the stage where you can identify the people, places, and things that should be in your reality. There is a choice, and tonight is the night to lock in self-empowerment.

First, set your timer for 10 minutes and complete your mirror work. This is a time to just observe yourself passively while you look in the mirror.

Next, write what comes through for you using the journaling prompts below.

Journaling prompts:
1. What goals have you not yet achieved?
2. Why do you judge yourself for it?
3. List five ways you can release attachment to where you should be and accept where you are.
4. Describe what you are thankful for in the present.

Bonus closing oracle spread: Tonight is about working through what the future holds for you. Consult the Intuitive Oracle Spread from the *Black Moon Lilith Cosmic Alchemy Oracle* for guidance.

NIGHT 11:
FULL EMBODIMENT WITH MULTIPLICATION

Aquarius is ascended knowledge when we are past 70 years old, and this time in life is when we are aware of how we fit into the social construct of society. The wisdom of age, innovation, humanitarianism, and the collective are all a part of this life cycle. This night is dedicated to how you can be of service to others while also staying true to your own unique purpose. It's also about how you can release the opinions and judgments you may receive for being your authentic self. Tonight, you will identify how your unique life purpose and role can help humanity. You also will look within to identify ways to remain consistent in your new way of being.

Multiplication is the alchemical phase where you make your new reality long-lasting by incorporating it into your life each day. This phase reminds you that action and consistency are required to change the unfavorable facets of your life and empower yourself. It's normal to stay in this phase for days, and then progress to the end when needed. You also can go through a repetition of the earlier stages to solidify and lock in the new ego you've identified over the past 10 days. You could support this by following courses each week toward a new career dream or by changing the way you talk to yourself and actively shifting your thought frequency. Spiritual shifts are not just ethereal things; they're also about what you do in your daily life over time.

You are finished with mirror work now. For these final days, we will focus on contemplative journaling and thoughtful reflection.

Next, write what comes through for you using the journaling prompts below.

Journaling prompts:
1. How have the opinions of others held you back from certain facets of your path?
2. How can you start to separate your truth from the opinions of others?
3. In what ways can you aid humanity through your purpose?

Bonus closing oracle spread: The Astrological Ancestral Healing Spread from the *Black Moon Lilith Cosmic Alchemy Oracle* will tap you into your mission and how it impacts the collective. It also will help clear any stagnant energies, like self-doubt, that can come from the outside world.

☿

NIGHT 12:
LIVING YOUR TRUTH WITH PROJECTION

Pisces is the end of the line and the final zodiac sign. It represents when we reach the end of our lives in old age if we are lucky, let go of the material world, and transcend into the spiritual.

In the projection phase, the inner state of being consciously reflects the outer one, and high-vibrational light is naturally projected into the world. Alchemy is a lifelong practice, but this is the phase where being in your truth is normal, natural, and easy for you.

As this process comes to a close, tonight's internal discussion is about how you can shine your light on this world, and about what to do in moments of self-doubt. After the current process is complete, always come back to this chapter in the book to revisit this energetic journey within.

Journaling prompts:
1. What are five things you are grateful for that have manifested into your reality since starting this workbook?
2. What are five things that were challenging for you to release?
3. What are five new habits and changes in your life that have been easy to maintain?
4. Write down what is no longer aligned and how you can change it.

Bonus closing oracle spread: The Cosmic Shadow Astrological Spread from the *Black Moon Lilith Cosmic Alchemy Oracle* is ideal for the reflective nature of tonight. Close your thought process by looking within at any remaining questions or concerns that were brought up in the night's work.

☿

NIGHT 13:
REFLECTION AND INTEGRATION

Now that you have gone on the full journey of under-standing the 12 alchemical processes, this is the day to reflect on each of your journal entries from the past 12 days. You may notice that you've written some raw, real, deep commentary about several areas and themes in your life. The power of this exercise is in going back over what you wrote and truly seeing how you converse with yourself and handle your reality. When you see the truth, it allows you to now choose a different option and strategy ahead.

Take this night to go back over each of the 12 days of your writings. Tonight, through the journaling prompts below, you will shine a light on the internal dialogue in your workbook entries. You will identify which parts of your own solutions you feel empowered to shift and implement into your life.

Final journaling prompts:
1. Take a look at and absorb your journal entries for each of the 12 days. Which were the most triggering or difficult for you to read?
2. On the other hand, which entries are more empowering and rest in the energy of the new, aligned version of yourself?
3. In your entries, what stood out as old patterns, limiting beliefs, and behaviors that are keeping you stuck in your life?
4. In your entries, what gave you emotions of joy, support, and harmony in your life?

Bonus closing oracle spread: Close out the entire ritual with the Alchemy Ascension Spread from the *Black Moon Lilith Cosmic Alchemy Oracle*. Each placement addresses the gates that you've experienced during this process. This will help you clarify remaining questions and help empower you on your life journey after the ritual.

⚸

Conclusion

EMBRACE YOUR POWER

While our time together is concluding, this is just the start of your empowering astrological and alchemical journey. Exploring the astrological significance of Black Moon Lilith can be a powerful tool for personal growth and healing. This dark and mysterious archetype can help us connect with the hidden aspects of ourselves, to reclaim our power, and to heal past wounds. By working with Black Moon Lilith, we can learn to embrace our primal instincts, to honor our desires, and to express ourselves authentically. We can also gain a deeper understanding of the ways in which we have been repressed, marginalized, or oppressed, and work to break free from these patterns.

There is an entire birth chart waiting to be discovered now that you have become an expert alchemist in transmuting your dark feminine power. Shadow work and integrating the knowledge of your birth chart is an ongoing practice through understanding how the planetary cycles and transits are affecting your present moment. I encourage you to revisit the wisdom you have just integrated when needed as you unpack the rest of your astrological chart.

Be prepared after you work with this book to recall the stories, allegory, and lessons mentioned in it as you go about your everyday life. In the future, you may feel yourself cry, purge, or feel empowered by what you've read. You may think back to triggers, aha moments, and learning lessons that were presented to you while you read the book; this is just a natural ascension symptom when you've learned transformative information. Energetic and emotional purges are healthy and encouraged.

Internal change can feel just as overwhelming as when it occurs in the physical, so be gentle with yourself going forward. I always advise my clients to use each of their days as a spiritual practice, taking them one at a time. By embracing the shadowy aspects of ourselves and connecting with the powerful, untamed energy of Black Moon Lilith, we can find healing and wholeness, and access our true potential as human beings.

☿

The Tropical Zodiac

Western astrology is an ancient divination system tracing back to approximately four thousand years ago in Mesopotamia. Modern society can only piece together its ancient origins from archeological evidence. The earliest evidence has been found in the ruins of ancient Mesopotamia, Greece, Rome, and Kemet (ancient Egypt). Over centuries, it traveled across the world due to colonization and conquering, and it evolved into what we know as modern astrology through astrological research, new planetary discoveries, and technological advances.

It's important to note that the astrology in this book is based on the tropical zodiac, which is used by most astrologers in the West. The seasons and the procession of the equinoxes determine the tropical zodiac versus the sidereal zodiac, which uses the constellations and fixed stars as a backdrop. In tropical, 0° Aries is the vernal point or spring equinox.

There are 12 signs in the zodiac. Each is represented by an archetype and rules over certain areas of life. When a planet moves into a zodiac sign, the planet operates with its qualities. Cardinal signs initiate the seasons, with the fixed signs grounded in the middle; the changeable, mutable signs are at the end. Aries is the astrological new year, starting the annual cycle at the spring equinox.

Each planet is also associated with one or two signs called the *planetary ruler*. A planet is at peak strength when it is moving through its own zodiac sign. Planets also easily exude the energy of the zodiac sign. Below is a general guide showing the 12 zodiac signs and the meaning, season, ruling planet, and symbol of each.

Sign	Season	Interpretation	Planetary Ruler	Symbol
Aries	March 21–April 19 (spring equinox)	*Cardinal.* Leading, active, self-assertive	Mars	the Ram
Taurus	April 20–May 20	*Fixed.* Stable, secure, sensual	Venus	the Bull
Gemini	May 21–June 20	*Mutable.* Communicative, versatile, sociable	Mercury	the Twins
Cancer	June 21–July 22 (summer solstice)	*Cardinal.* Sensitive, nurturing, protective	Moon	the Crab
Leo	July 23–August 22	*Fixed.* Creative, loyal, regal	Sun	the Lion
Virgo	August 23–September 22	*Mutable.* Work-oriented, productive, analytical	Mercury	the Maiden

Libra	September 23–October 22 (fall equinox)	*Cardinal.* Social, loves beauty, partnership-oriented	Venus	the Scales
Scorpio	October 23–November 21	*Fixed.* Intense, passionate, regenerative	Mars and Pluto	the Scorpion
Sagittarius	November 22–December 21	*Mutable.* Adventurous, optimistic, philosophical	Jupiter	the Archer
Capricorn	December 22–January 19 (winter solstice)	*Cardinal.* Responsible, disciplined, motivated	Saturn	the Sea Goat
Aquarius	January 20–February 18	*Fixed.* Eclectic, nonconformist, detached	Saturn and Uranus	the Water Bearer
Pisces	February 19–March 20	*Mutable.* Emotional, imaginative, self-sacrificing	Jupiter and Neptune	the Fish

☿

APPENDIX 2

The 12 Houses

In astrology, the circular 360° chart is divided into 12 pie-shaped sections called the *houses*. You can think of them as where the planets live in your chart and what area of life their transit will affect. Understanding which planets and signs are in certain houses in your chart can explain the how, when, and where. Each house is also associated with a different facet of life. Here is a guide below to each house, related zodiac sign, and what area of life is affected.

The 12 Houses	Interpretation	Related Sign
1st House	Self, identity, personality	Aries
2nd House	Finances, money, self-worth	Taurus
3rd House	Communication, siblings, writing	Gemini
4th House	Home, family, emotions	Cancer
5th House	Self-expression, romance, children	Leo
6th House	Health, routine, work	Virgo
7th House	Relationships, contracts, marriage	Libra
8th House	Sex, death, investments	Scorpio
9th House	Publishing, international travel, law	Sagittarius
10th House	Career, public image, prestige	Capricorn
11th House	Groups, friends, wishes	Aquarius
12th House	Seclusion, subconscious, secrets	Pisces

♃

The Planets, Points, and Asteroids

The planets, points, and asteroids are extremely important because they indicate more information about how and what will manifest. Each planet is interpreted differently and governs certain archetypes, places, things, and situations. Planets and asteroids are the celestial bodies that move through space. Even though the sun and moon are grouped with the planets, they are luminaries. Points are important cusps or intersections in the natal chart that rule over specific areas of life. Below are the different major planets, points, and asteroids in astrology with their interpretations.

Planet, Placement, or Asteroid	Interpretation
Sun	Self, ego, life force
Moon	Soul, instincts, emotions
Mercury	Communication, thought, mental energy
Venus	Relationships, money, pleasure
Mars	Action, passion, drive
Jupiter	Expansion, luck, optimism
Saturn	Discipline, delay, lessons
Uranus	Shocks, revolution, technology
Neptune	Illusion, loss, imagination
Pluto	Death, crisis, change
North and South Nodes of the Moon	Life destiny, karmic direction, release
Black Moon Lilith	Rage, rebellion, self-undoing
Pallas Athena	Wisdom, war, crafts, teaching, writing
Juno	Long-term relationships, loyalty, betrayal, devotion
Ceres	Motherhood, nurturing, food, separation
Chiron	Deep wounds, healing power

BENEFIC AND MALEFIC PLANETS

A benefic planet is one that is believed to bring positive influences and good fortune to a person's life. The two most considered benefic planets in traditional Western astrology are Jupiter and Venus, which are associated with expansion, abundance, prosperity, love, and harmony. The moon is also sometimes considered a benefic planet, where it is associated with emotional well-being, maternal nurturing, and intuition.

A malefic planet is one that is believed to bring negative influences and challenges to a person's life. The two most considered malefic planets in traditional Western astrology are Saturn and Mars, which are associated with limitations, obstacles, and conflict.

☿

APPENDIX 4

Major Planetary Aspects, Elements, Angles, and Polarities

PLANETARY ASPECTS

Aspects are the connections between the planets, points, and asteroids—they are the lines you see on a transit or natal chart. Each connection holds a different vibration and indicates positive change, evolution, or disruption. Below are the major planetary aspects and how to interpret them in a chart.

Aspect	Degrees	Soft or Hard Aspect	Interpretation
Conjunction	0 or 360°	Neutral	A powerful connection in one zodiac sign
Opposition	180°	Hard	The need to balance and integrate opposing forces
Trine	120°	Soft	Positive energy flow between planets
Sextile	60°	Soft	An easy and harmonious exchange
Square	90°	Hard	A harsh connection representing conflict and change

ANGLES

The angles in astrology are extremely important hot spots. They are not planets—they mark the cusp, or beginning, of the first, fourth, seventh, and tenth houses. Each represents an important facet of life, and when they are activated by planets, asteroids, or points, you will see their archetypes manifest. Below is a guide to each angle and how to interpret it.

Angle	Interpretation
Ascendant	Cusp of first house. Your identity, personal appearance, self
Descendant	Cusp of seventh house. Relationships, marriage, business partnerships, agreements
Imum Coeli (IC)	Cusp of fourth house. Ancestry, lineage, home, the parent
Medium Coeli (MC) or Midheaven	Cusp of tenth house. Career, public image, prestige, the parent

ELEMENTS AND POLARITIES

The four mystical elements in astrology indicate how a zodiac sign operates. Masculine or feminine signs in astrology have nothing to do with what gender you identify as. Understanding how much masculine or feminine energy is in your chart can help you live a more aligned life. The elements describe the nature of a sign and how it moves in this physical reality. Masculine signs (fire and air) are externally driven and active. Feminine signs (water and earth) are more receptive and seek energy internally. Below is a guide to each element, along with whether it is of masculine or feminine energy.

Element	Signs	Polarity	Interpretation
Fire	Aries, Leo, Sagittarius	Masculine / Active	Creative, optimistic, energetically vibrant
Air	Libra, Gemini, Aquarius	Masculine / Active	Logical, communicative, cerebral
Earth	Virgo, Taurus, Capricorn	Feminine / Receptive	Practical, sensorial, grounded
Water	Scorpio, Cancer, Pisces	Feminine / Receptive	Emotional, intuitive, creative

♉

APPENDIX 5

Placidus House System

The Placidus house system is a widely used, time-based astrological house system that divides the ecliptic, the sun's apparent path into the 12 houses. Its foundation is found in the *Tetrabiblios,* a tome by the ancient astrologer Ptolemy in Alexandrian Egypt around second A.D. However, it's theorized that it goes back much further than that. It evolved and was later named after Italian astrologer, mathematician, and monk Placidus de Titis, who took and expanded Ptolemy's work in the 1600s.

To simplify, in the Placidus system, the ascendant and midheaven are determined by a complex set of calculations that consider the latitude and longitude of the birthplace. This means that the size and shape of the houses can vary and include more than one zodiac sign.

The Placidus system is one of the most popular and widely used house systems in astrology, particularly in Western astrology. It is believed to provide a more accurate and detailed picture of a person's life and personality than some of the other house systems, such as the equal house system or the whole sign house system. However, like all house systems, the Placidus system is based on a set of assumptions and principles that may not be accepted by all astrologers, and its accuracy and usefulness may vary depending on the individual chart and the astrologer's interpretation.

♃

APPENDIX 6

Precession of the Equinoxes

In astronomy and astrology, the precession of the equinoxes refers to the gradual shift of the equinoxes along the ecliptic (the apparent path of the sun in the sky as seen from Earth). The equinoxes are the two points on the ecliptic where the plane of the Earth's equator intersects with the ecliptic, and they mark the beginning of spring (the vernal equinox) and autumn (the autumnal equinox).

Due to the gravitational pull of the moon and the sun on Earth's equatorial bulge, Earth's rotational axis wobbles like a spinning top, which causes the position of the equinoxes to shift gradually over time. This means that the tropical zodiac, which is based on the position of the sun relative to the equinoxes, also shifts gradually over time.

The precession of the equinoxes has important implications for astrology because it affects the way that astrologers calculate the positions of the planets and other celestial bodies in the birth chart. In Western astrology, for example, astrologers use the tropical zodiac, which is based on the position of the sun relative to the equinoxes, to determine the sign placements of the planets and other points in the chart. However, because the position of the equinoxes is shifting gradually over time, the positions of the signs in the tropical zodiac are slowly drifting away from their original positions relative to the constellations of the zodiac. This means that the zodiac sign placements in a birth chart may not correspond exactly to the positions of the constellations in the sky.

To account for this, some astrologers use the sidereal zodiac, which is based on the actual positions of the constellations in the sky, rather than the tropical zodiac. However, the use of the sidereal zodiac is not universally accepted in Western astrology, and there is ongoing debate among astrologers about the best way to account for the precession of the equinoxes in astrological calculations.

⚵

Endnotes

1. *Encyclopedia Britannica*, "Lilith," accessed April 3, 2023. https://www.britannica.com/topic/Lilith-Jewish-folklore.

2. "Statuette of a veiled and masked dancer," British Museum, accessed April 13, 2023, https://www.britishmuseum.org/collection/object/W_2003-0718-1.

3. Ivy Goldstein-Jacobson and Delphine Jay, *Dark Moon Lilith in Astrology* (Kessinger Publishing, 2010).

4. Alastair Smart, "Picasso 50 Years on: Greatest Artist of the 20th Century, or Cancel-Worthy Misogynist?," *The Independent*. https://www.independent.co.uk/artsentertainment/art/features/picasso-50-years-exhibition-b2303086.html

5. Liz Fields, "The Story Behind Billie Holiday's 'Strange Fruit,'" American Masters, April 12, 2021, accessed October 21, 2022. https://www.pbs.org/wnet/americanmasters/the-story-behind-billie-holidays-strange-fruit/17738/

6. Greta Thunberg, Twitter post, August 31, 2019, accessed October 21, 2023, https://twitter.com/GretaThunberg/status/1167916177927991296?lang=en

7. Jolie Solomon, "Overlooked No More: Louise Little, Activist and Mother of Malcolm X," *The New York Times*, March 19, 2022, accessed October 21, 2022. https://www.nytimes.com/2022/03/19/obituaries/louise-little-overlooked.html

8. "Jennifer Aniston's Mom: Everything to Know about Her Late Mother & Their Infamous Feud," Hollywood Life, accessed October 21, 2022, https://hollywoodlife.com/feature/jennifer-aniston-mom-4642884.

9. "Jennifer Aniston Reveals Struggles with Dyslexia," *The Hollywood Reporter*, Jan 21, 2015, accessed October 21, 2022. https://www.hollywoodreporter.com/news/general-news/jennifer-aniston-reveals-struggles-dyslexia-764854/

10. Steve Inskeep, "The Singular Woman Who Raised Barack Obama," NPR, May 3, 2011, https://www.npr.org/2011/05/03/135840068/the-singular-woman-who-raised-barack-obama.

11. Jeff Zeleny and Jim Rutenberg, "Obama Sharply Assails Absent Black Fathers " *The New York Times*, June 16, 2008, doi: https://www.nytimes.com/2008/06/16/us/politics/15cnd-obama.html.

12. Royce Dunmore, "Lizzo Responds to Kanye West after He Fat-Shamed Her: 'I'm Minding My Fat, Black, Beautiful Business'," BET, August 11, 2021, https://www.bet.com/article/j13hy6/lizzo-responds-ye-after-he-fat-shamed-her-im-minding-my-fat-black-beautiful-business.

13. Emily McCombs, "Why Lizzo's Health Is None of Your Business," HuffPost, August 20, 2021, https://www.huffpost.com/entry/concern-trolling-lizzo-health-weight_l_611d8650e4b0caf7ce2c8a17.

14. Giles Hattersley, "Lizzo: 'I'm Going to Make You My Hype Girl'," *Vogue UK*, December 2, 2019, https://www.vogue.co.uk/article/lizzo-singer-interview-2019.

15. Jon Blistein, "Lizzo Plays 'America the Beautiful' on Crystal-Covered Flute at James Madison's Montpelier," *Rolling Stone*, September 18, 2021, https://www.rollingstone.com/music/music-news/lizzo-plays-james-madison-crystal-flute-1234601617/.

16. Marybeth Gasman, "Why Lizzo Playing a Flute from the Library of Congress Is Important," *Forbes*, October 2, 2022, https://www.forbes.com/sites/marybethgasman/2022/10/02/why-lizzo-playing-a-flute-from-the-library-of-congress-is-important/.

17. Chris Willman, "Lizzo's James Madison Flute Performance at GOP Event Sends Republicans into a Rage," *Variety*, September 26, 2022, https://variety.com/2022/music/news/lizzo-james-madison-flute-republicans-furious-1235389304/.

18. "Lizzo," *Biography*, accessed October 21, 2022, https://www.
    biography.com/musician/lizzo.

19. "Trauma Partners," video, Facebook, January 26, 2022, https://www.
    facebook.com/unfilteredonwatch/videos/310307613463046/.

20. Danuta Kean, "Hugh Hefner, Playboy Founder, Dies at 91,"
    The Guardian, September 28, 2017, accessed October 21,
    2022, https://www.theguardian.com/media/2017/sep/28/
    hugh-hefner-playboy-founder-91-dark-side.

21. Sara Kettler, "The Infamous Tonya Harding and Nancy Kerrigan
    Scandal: A Timeline," *Biography*, January 31, 2020, accessed
    October 21, 2022, https://www.biography.com/news/
    tonya-harding-nancy-kerrigan-attack-photos.

22. "Bill & Melinda Gates Foundation—Warren Buffett," The Giving
    Pledge, accessed October 21, 2022, https://givingpledge.org/
    pledger?pledgerId=177.

23. Taylor Locke, "Warren Buffet Is 'Halfway' through Giving Away His
    Massive Forture. Here's Why His Kids Will Get Almost None of His
    $100 Billion," CNBC, June 23, 2021, accessed October 21, 2022,
    https://www.cnbc.com/2021/06/23/why-warren-buffett-isnt
    -leaving-his-100-billion-dollar-fortune-to-his-kids.html.

☿

Bibliography

Brady, Bernadette. *Brady's Book of Fixed Stars*. York, ME: Samuel Weiser, 1998.

Hurwitz, Siegmund. *Lilith: The First Eve*. Einsiedeln, Switzerland: Daimon Verlag, 2009.

Jay, Delphine Gloria. *Interpreting Lilith*. Tempe, AZ: American Federation of Astrologers, 1981.

———. *The Lilith Ephemeris 1900–2000 AD*. Tempe, AZ: American Federation of Astrologers, 1983.

———. *The Lilith Ephemeris 2000–2050 AD*. Tempe, AZ: American Federation of Astrologers, 2011.

Johnson, Alfred Sydney. Clarence A. Bickford, William W. Hudson, and Nathan Haskell Dole, eds. *The Cyclopedic Review of Current History*. Vol. 8. Detroit: Current History Company, 1898.

Michelsen, Neil F. *The Asteroid Ephemeris 1900 to 2050*. San Diego: ACS Publications, 1999.

———. *The American Ephemeris for the 21st Century: 2000 to 2050 at Noon*. San Diego: ACS Publications, 1996.

———. *The American Ephemeris for the 20th Century: 1900 to 2000 at Midnight*. San Diego: ACS Publications, 1991.

Santoni, Francis. "Ephemeris of the Black Moon 1910–2010." In *The Black Moon Book*, by Francis Santoni, Demetra George, and Lee A. Suyterman. Fairfield, IA: Sum Press, 1994.

Schmadel, Lutz D. *Dictionary of Minor Planet Names*. Berlin: Springer, 2012.

Three Initiates. *The Kybalion: A Study of the Hermetic Philosophy of Ancient Egypt and Greece*. Chicago: The Yogi Publication Society, 1908.

Acknowledgments

No one walks a path alone, and I have been blessed with family, friends, teachers, clients, and mentors who have helped me along the way.

I first want to acknowledge you as a reader of this book. Thank you for allowing me into your sacred astrological healing journey. I especially want to thank my Black Moon Lilith Collective tribe members on LilithAstrology .com who have supported my work over the years, believing in the power of the dark goddess. Thank you to you and every follower, reader, and client over the years who has supported my work. I feel grateful for this platform and the opportunity to share my voice and perspective.

To my parents, who always encouraged and made space for my creative spirit and "out-there" ideas. To the lioness matriarchs of my family who've inspired my work.

To my cherished chosen family, friends, colleagues, and collaborators over the years who were always there to assist, share advice, make me laugh, and listen to my latest horoscope; who booked readings, recommended my practice, collaborated, and supported my work. Special mention to Ronnie Peters, Matthew Stopera, Virginia Moore,

Kevin Smith, Courtney Latter, Baze Mpinja, Glennis Meagher, Ilana Glazer, Whitney Jefferson, Dorsey Shaw, Colin Bedell, Nadiya Shah, Lars Mellis, Stephanie Campos, Laura Chung, and Rae Fagin.

To Ruby Warrington: this work would not have come to life without your friendship, wisdom and fairy-godmother magic. Thank you for the coffee dates, lunch meetups, and endless support during my writing journey.

To my teachers, mentors, and colleagues at the National Council for Geocosmic Research for teaching me the professionalism, accuracy, and knowledge required to be a professional astrologer. From workshops and conferences to classes, I would not be the astrologer I am today without the solid education from this organization. Special mention to my private teacher and mentor, Meira Epstein.

To my literary agent, Coleen O'Shea; editor Anna Cooperberg, and the Hay House team: thank you for believing in the magical power of Lilith.

About the Author

Adama Sesay is a professional astrologer, occultist, entrepreneur, and author of *Black Moon Lilith Rising* and *Black Moon Lilith Cosmic Alchemy Oracle*. She studied the metaphysical science of astrology through the National Council for Geocosmic Research and is a self-taught tarot and oracle card reader. She has been playing professionally in the mystical, spiritual, beauty, and fashion industries since 2010. Her astrological writing is featured in major outlets like *Cosmopolitan*, BuzzFeed, Byrdie, *Allure*, *Essence*, Today.com, Astrology.com, and Well+Good.

In 2019, Adama gave birth to LilithAstrology.com, an esoteric media brand dedicated to empowering humanity through the dark divine feminine goddess Lilith. She is the host of the *Black Moon Lilith Rising* podcast and runs the empowering private streaming platform Black Moon Lilith Collective. She holds consultations and events globally, with notable and celebrity clients.

About the Illustrator

Carlos Fama is a highly skilled mixed-media digital artist who was born in Spain. With a passion for creativity and innovation, he utilizes his expertise to produce stunning digital artwork that captivates and inspires audiences around the world. His dynamic range of artistic styles, combined with his attention to detail and mastery of various digital tools and techniques make him a sought-after artist in the industry. Fama's work has been featured in numerous exhibitions, galleries, and publications, and he continues to push the boundaries of digital art with his imaginative and cutting-edge pieces.

Hay House Titles of Related Interest

YOU CAN HEAL YOUR LIFE, the movie,
starring Louise Hay & Friends
(available as an online streaming video)
www.hayhouse.com/louise-movie

THE SHIFT, the movie,
starring Dr. Wayne W. Dyer
(available as an online streaming video)
www.hayhouse.com/the-shift-movie

***

*AFRICAN GODDESS INITIATION: Sacred Rituals for Self-Love,
Prosperity, and Joy,* by Abiola Abrams

*AFRICAN GODDESS RISING ORACLE: A 44-Card Deck and
Guidebook,* by Abiola Abrams

*WHAT'S YOUR SOUL SIGN?: Astrology for Waking Up,
Transforming, and Living a High-Vibe Life,* by Debbie Frank

*YOU ARE A GODDESS: Working with the Sacred Feminine to
Awaken, Heal, and Transform,* by Sophie Bashford

All of the above are available at www.hayhouse.co.uk.

***

CONNECT WITH
HAY HOUSE
ONLINE

🌐 hayhouse.co.uk   **f** @hayhouse

📷 @hayhouseuk   **𝕏** @hayhouseuk

▶ @hayhouseuk   ♪ @hayhouseuk

Find out all about our latest books & card decks • Be the first to know about exclusive discounts • Interact with our authors in live broadcasts • Celebrate the cycle of the seasons with us • Watch free videos from your favourite authors • Connect with like-minded souls

'*The gateways to wisdom and knowledge are always open.*'

Louise Hay